Journey into Friendship

Megan M. Drummond
and
Jessica Denise McFarlane

AmErica House
Baltimore

First printing

ISBN: 1-58851-116-2
PUBLISHED BY AMERICA HOUSE BOOK
PUBLISHERS
www.publishamerica.com
Baltimore

Printed in the United States of America

I dedicate this book to my loving, supportive family and friends who believed in me.

- JDM

* * *

This book is for all my friends and family who've always been there and supported me in everything.

- MMD

Introduction
by Megan and Jessica

Close friendships are among the most important relationships a person can have. Friends are always there to talk, to laugh, to cry and often to share some of life's most important moments with you. A person can often confide to his or her closest friends' things that they can't talk to their parents, siblings or even spouses about. In the pages that follow, you will read about two best friends who traveled the winding path from teenagers to women together. Their journey has had its ups and downs, its difficult times and its triumphs. Through all the twists and turns, however, these women developed and kept a deep friendship intact and brought a greater sense of themselves out of the experience. Despite physical disabilities, they survived college and discovered much about life and a lot about themselves.

* * * * *

After Jessica and I wrote the above, rather melodramatic, introduction, we decided to put a more real explanation of how this book came to be in the introduction.

When we started writing this in the summer of 1998, we had only the intention of writing it as a "memory book." We wanted to have something to look back on in 20 years and remember our years in college together. Memories and even pictures fade after time, but the written word stays forever.

Jessica and I started this project with absolutely no intention of getting it published. We joked around with the idea but neither of us was serious about it. Shortly after my 22nd birthday, we decided to start trying to find a publisher. Jessica had gotten me some books about friendships between women for my birthday and after I read them and told her about them, we figured the book that what we were writing was just as interesting. And more in-depth, because it focuses on only one set of friends instead of little snippets of many different friendships.

A year and a half later, when I received word that someone was going to give this book a shot at publication, we decided that it could serve a purpose other than sharing a story of friends. *Journey Into Friendship* may also help dispel a few stereotypes that people still hold about those with disabilities. In our many and varied experiences, we have encountered people who seem to think that life with a disability is not worth living. Some think that a person with a disability can't do anything, is incapable of even getting a college education. Still others seem to think that the life of a disabled person is totally filled with complications, one big problem, or on the other end of the spectrum, that it is completely uncomplicated by anything.

These are in no way, shape or form, true. Our lives are just like anyone else's lives. We go to school, work, play, date and the life of a person with a disability is far from being problem-free.

So, now that you know why we wrote this book and what we hope to accomplish with it, we hope you enjoy *Journey Into Friendship.*

About My Best Friend
by Megan

I first met Jessica McFarlane on August 28, 1994, when she wheeled into my room and asked me to go to the freshman mixer with her. I wasn't quite sure what to think of her. I had seen her off and on all that day while my parents and brother were setting up my room. But I hadn't met her yet.

I agreed to go over with her and that night started a lasting friendship. Over the four years that we were in school together, I learned a lot about Jessica. In a few of our conversations, I learned more about her than I ever wanted to know. She had to explain every little detail about her disability to me because I hadn't been around a lot of people with disabilities before.

Jessica has a condition known as cerebral palsy, more commonly referred to as CP. CP is caused by an injury to the developing brain or the newly developed brain. It is not hereditary, but the injury that results in cerebral palsy can be caused by a lack of oxygen to the brain, complications during birth, or a sickness passed from the mother to the baby during pregnancy. In Jessica's case, the doctors and the hospital made several mistakes during her birth that led to a lack of oxygen to her brain.

Her parents did not know that Jessica had cerebral palsy until she was three years old. Her doctors led them to believe that their daughter was simply progressing slowly and that she would soon catch up to her peers. They did not want to admit that something they had done might have caused Jessica to have a permanent physical disability.

The severity and type of cerebral palsy depend on the location of the brain damage and to what extent the area was damaged. Jessica has a combination of types. Athetoid means the messages her brain sends to her muscles usually get mixed up along the way, causing involuntary movements. Sometimes, though, her muscles get very stiff. This is known as spasticity. The CP also affects Jessica's speech. Her speech is sometimes slurred and she has to stop frequently to swallow or clear her throat. She is almost always understandable, though.

Jessica went to a special kindergarten that was a two-hour round trip bus ride from her home for therapy and early intervention. When she did start school, she started in a different school that was still a two-hour round trip from her home. This school had classes for special needs children that her home district did not have. She was placed in a special education classroom. Jessica was very bright and did not need to be in this class, but she was placed in it because the school closer to her home was not prepared for a disabled student in the mainstream. She remained here through fourth grade.

In this class, she would finish her own work early and then help the other students with theirs. She would help them with such tasks as learning the alphabet and numbers, or help them solve simple math problems. This experience planted the seed for her wanting to become a special education teacher. When she started fifth grade, her parents had gotten Jessica placed in the mainstream with the rest of her class. Because mainstreaming and inclusion were such a new idea in the early 80s, Jessica had to prove to her teachers and friends that she belonged in a regular class. She remained mainstreamed throughout junior high and high school.

During her high school years, Jessica continued her tutoring activities. She would often go and help the younger children in the special education classes. She helped the kids with difficult assignments, worked to get them to communicate better, and assisted the teacher whenever she could. Jessica also added disability awareness to her activities. In high school, she organized a day to help the other kids understand her CP and wrote articles for the school paper to help the other students understand disabilities.

When she started college, Jessica had no doubt that she wanted to be a teacher. Lots of people at Edinboro University have been supportive of her decision and have tried to help her in any way they can. A few of her professors have tried to discourage her from teaching, though. This negative attitude has only strengthened her resolve.

There have been a few that have tried to discourage her from even being in college, though. The most notable was a philosophy professor we both had. He did not want a student with a disability in his class. He didn't know either of us and had no knowledge of what we could do academically. Like many people, he only saw the physical limitations and equated that to intellectual limitations. He did not think that Jessica could handle the work and guaranteed her a D in the course no matter how good her actual work. After much contemplation, she chose not to endanger her QPA. She filed a formal discrimination complaint against him and transferred into another philosophy class, where she earned a B with very little effort.

Jessica successfully completed both of her field experiences and her student teaching. In some ways, her disability has been as asset in the field, allowing an easy transition into lessons on different types of people, helping, and listening. Jessica graduated with her degree in special education in December of 1998. She plans to get her Master's degree in special education or counseling and school psychology.

About My Best Friend
by Jessica

I met Megan Drummond on moving day at Edinboro University on August 28, 1994. Megan was also a freshman and lived two dorm rooms down from mine. I had just turned 19 and she would be turning 18 in a few days. My parents pushed me to introduce myself to her because I wanted to meet new friends. The first thing I noticed about Megan was her love for country music. I could not stand country. She had posters of various country singers hanging on her walls and country music playing on her stereo. From that moment, I knew we were going to have a fascinating friendship.

Megan did not always have a disability. She grew up healthy for the first seven years of life. That all changed in the blink of an eye. When she was seven, she woke up one July morning and felt like she had the flu. She got out of bed and literally crawled to the bathroom, and Megan became increasingly sick. She could hardly walk and felt miserable. Her mother had to carry Megan to the car and took her to the doctor's. He examined her and sent her to the hospital, saying she was dehydrated. They treated her at the local hospital as best they could.

Unfortunately, dehydration was not the problem. Later that day, an ambulance transported her to Buffalo Children's Hospital. By the next morning, Megan was in a coma-like state. No one knew what was happening to her. She would wake and sleep, but could not respond to anything. She stayed this way for three weeks.

When Megan came out of the coma-like state, she could not physically do anything. She could not speak, use her limbs or control her bathroom needs. Luckily, her mental abilities were not affected. Megan had to be fed through a tube and needed constant care. She had to stay in the hospital for seven weeks. Through time and therapy, Megan slowly gained back her skills. She began to communicate with a board with words on it. She could eat normally again. The best explanation doctors had was that Megan had suffered a stroke. A cerebrovascular accident, or stroke, occurs when an artery leading to or in the brain is blocked or breaks. They were not sure then and they are not certain now that she definitely had a stroke. A stroke is extremely unusual at such a young age.

Megan stayed at a rehabilitation hospital to further her physical progress. Her parents wanted her to regain as much of her independence as possible. Emotionally this was a difficult decision on her and her parents. Megan would be a few hours away from her home. Her parents, however, took her home just about every weekend. The rehabilitation did pay off because Megan gained back total use of her left arm and bathroom needs.

Megan can now feed herself, write and do most things by herself. She can walk with help or the use of grab bars. Megan does need help with some minor things, but mainly she is independent. With speech therapy, Megan was able to speak again. She speaks very softly and sometimes her words are slurred together. The more you know her, the easier it is to understand her. Nothing irritates us more than when someone does not understand us, but they act like they do. It is much better to ask the person to repeat him or herself instead of making an assumption. Megan had schooling in the rehabilitation hospital. She did not want to fall behind in school.

When she got out of the hospital and before she went into rehab, she was home tutored. Megan was very smart and it did not take her long to catch up with her class. When she returned to school in the fifth grade, Megan had a full time aide to help with physical needs. For a brief time, the school placed Megan in a special education class. She was a little slower than the rest of her class when doing math, but was taken out of the special education class as soon as she caught up.

Megan graduated with her class in June 1994. Many people did not think Megan would graduate on time, but she proved them wrong. Megan's main interests were reading and writing. She also liked children. So when she started college, she wasn't sure what she wanted to be. Megan chose to be an English major. Then as time went on she thought she like to teach pre-school. The preschool degree was only an associates. She and her dad wanted Megan to have a four-year degree. So, she then chose elementary education. Megan is a quiet and calm person. She is not very loud and hyper. Megan thought it over and realized teaching was not her thing. After she tried her hand at psychology, she settled on an English major. She also excelled at it.

During Megan's senior year at Edinboro, she became involved in writing for the school newspaper. She wrote a few articles for the college's online newspaper as well. Megan took a few journalism courses as well. She wanted an internship in the fall of 1998, but due to some financial problems, she could not do one.

Megan and I planned on graduating together in December 1998, but she was forced to take her last course in the summer of 1998. Megan wants to be a writer, but is looking for any job with writing in it for the time being. Currently, Megan is working for a disability service agency in a Public Relations position located in Bradford, Pennsylvania. One day, she hopes to get her Master's degree in English or a related field.

The Beginnings
Of Friendship
by Jessica

Starting college brings forth many emotions. Sadness, excitement, fear and anticipation are just some emotions experienced by college students. College freshmen deal with some exceptionally strong feelings as they enter college. They have new responsibilities, friends, influences and professors. The homework load is more difficult compared with senior high. Many college students move out of their homes for the first time. Whatever the case may be for a student, the college experience is one that will be difficult to forget.

The feelings of responsibility, nervousness and excitement often triple when the college freshman has a physical disability. A student with a disability has many things to remember and think about when going to college. Many people assume that because a student has a physical disability, there is no way they can attend college. That might have been true 30 or more years ago, but not anymore. People with disabilities are capable of making a life for themselves. Just because a physical problem exists does not mean that someone has a mental disability.

Having a disability causes challenges. Challenges are

a good thing because they make life more interesting. No matter what the challenge, with a little determination, people with disabilities can reach their goals. Living at college might take some adjustment. If a student has a severe disability and is used to being cared for by family members, the transition to college is often more difficult. The student needs to rely on others, express themselves well and try to be as independent as possible. The student is in charge of his or her life and must express any needs to the faculty and friends.

I felt many emotions when I began college. My feelings ranged from fear to sheer excitement for the challenge. Moving day, my freshman year, fell on the day after my nineteenth birthday. August 28, 1994. I had looked forward to going to college ever since I was a little girl. When I was in the eighth grade a teacher told my parents and me about Edinboro. My dad automatically turned off the idea, but I felt determined to go. Living six hours away sounded thrilling. I always enjoyed learning and felt that college was a necessary step in my life. I felt apprehensive, but ready for any upcoming challenges that lay ahead. Little did I know just how many challenges that I would face and ultimately conquer. Due to my experiences, however, I matured and college life helped shape the person I am today.

I use a motorized purple wheelchair to get around, but I can walk with some assistance by another person. Like many individuals with CP, I need assistance in daily care routines such as dressing, feeding, toileting and other daily living tasks. I try to do these things on my own, but my muscles are not cooperative. Sometimes it feels like my limbs are two-year old children that each want to do their own thing. When my muscles do not cooperate, I feel frustrated, but I just go with the flow. When I began college, I felt nervous relying on others taking care of me. However, before I went to Edinboro, I researched the disability program thoroughly and knew I would get quality care. I was very satisfied when I learned that the care did live up to my expectations.

When I began at Edinboro University of Pennsylvania, I knew two people who attended also and wondered who else I would meet. Another girl from my high school started Edinboro the same time that I did. We were not friends though, just acquaintances. There was also a woman from my church who went to Edinboro. She was a senior, but she did tell me a lot about Edinboro and I could call her if I needed anything.

I am not too shy once I actually meet and get to know someone. I'm not as outgoing as I would like, but college made me more outgoing. At college, I learned to smile more and start conversations with others. I planned to be more outgoing and not let cerebral palsy dictate my social life. No matter who you are, people often judge you based on your appearance. When a person has a physical disability, it is right there for the world to see. The challenge is getting people to see past the disability. As you can probably imagine, this is a lot easier said than done. I, like many people with physical disabilities, want the world to see the real person inside and not the object of a cane, wheelchair or other assistive devices.

The first day of college, everyone moves into their dorm room or apartment. As a freshman at Edinboro, a student must live in the dorm for two semesters. This is so they can have a taste of living on their own and have limited supervision under residence life. I decided to live in the dorm all of college because of personal care and places were more accessible.

The dorm I was assigned to was called Scranton Hall. My dorm room, A 20, had a construction paper green balloon taped to the door with my name on it. I felt depressed as I entered the seemingly empty and uninviting room. My dorm was a standard dorm with two closets, two dressers, a twin bed and one window. When my parents started to move my stuff in, I began to feel much better because it was looking more like my room at home.

After we bought a carpet at Sears, my parents helped me unpack and set up my room. My carpet was soft and off white. We found it fairly quickly and it covered the floor almost entirely. By the fifth year of college, amazingly the carpet looked great and someone bought it from me for their dining room. Being that my parents are divorced, working together brought about some tense moments, but somehow we survived. Setting up the room was also a stressful situation because we live so far away. My parents and I wanted to make it right the first time. They could not drive up again just like that to fix the problem.

My room arrangement differs from that of the average person or wheelchair user. For greater independence, I need my things placed on the floor for me to use. I find that I have much more stability on the floor. I crawl to get around, and I also type faster. Being on the floor helps keep my muscles flexible, and I get exercise. I do not foresee myself living most of my life on the floor at 40, but you never know. My computer, stereo, bed and books all need to be lower so I can use them myself. With everything lower, I am much more independent. Whenever someone went by my room or entered, they always had to take a second look because of the different arrangement.

The college permits students to do whatever they need to make their dorm room the most accessible and comfortable for their needs. However, you could not mess with the electrical wires, but I never understood why you would want to. Painting your room is possible. I wanted to paint my room purple, but obviously my parents did not have the time to paint. So, I settled for a beige room. When setting up a room, independence for the student is, of course, the key factor and not the appearance. I covered the walls with calendars, posters, and pictures and had an array of knickknacks on the shelves. My bed had many stuffed animals that the personal care workers had fun arranging each morning.

I helped my parents unpack by directing them where to put my things. The amount of belongings a student can fit into a dorm room is truly amazing. I also didn't have a roommate, so I could not even imagine having to fit two people's items in the room. I over packed, of course. It took me all four years to know how much I needed to pack. My motto was better safe than sorry. My dad's motto was less is best. I heard Edinboro had very cold weather so I believe I packed every sweater and turtleneck that I owned.

During arranging my room, I thought about my

happiness living six hours away from my family. I already missed my boyfriend, dog, and family. I longed for my bedroom and house. College looked less and less appealing. Am I going to fit in and make friends? How will I survive by myself? The simple answer had to be yes because I wanted to be a teacher and succeed on my own. I knew it wouldn't be easy, but I could make it.

Earlier that day, I had heard about a Welcome Back Dance in the University Center at 8:00 for the college students. I have always enjoyed dances. In high school, I went to several dances with friends and alone. I wanted to go to this dance, but I wanted someone to go with me. I would feel out of place and lonely. My parents and I discussed the dance off and on. They were trying to persuade me to go. They said that most of the people at the dance would feel out of place and lonely. They reminded me that the purpose of the dance was to meet people. Despite their persuasion, I wanted to find another freshman to talk and maybe to go to the dance with me. I wanted a freshman because they could relate to my feelings and apprehensions of college life.

Scranton Hall's entire first floor, at the time, consisted of women who are physically disabled and need some kind of physical assistance. In the dorm next to Scranton, Shafer Hall, the first floor is devoted to men with physical disabilities. These physical needs may include dressing, showering, and doing hair or any other assistance. Personal care attendants are always on the floor 24 hours a day to help with these needs.

On our floor, I could not determine who was a freshman. Some girls, however, looked as scared as I was. Up the hallway, in room A 16, lived a young woman who my mom thought was a freshman too. I was not sure. She confused me at first because she did not look like a woman. She had really short blond hair and was tall. Then again, I only zipped by her once or twice. I did not get a good look at her. I noticed she had a fancy wheelchair. With controls, she could make the seat rise up and down for when she wants to reach something up high. The legs can also go up and down to improve circulation in her legs. My wheelchair just moves forward, backward, left and right.

The dance was only a few hours away. My parents finally persuaded me to go introduce myself to the young woman who lived in room 16. I went down to her room after her parents left. She looked a little sad as most people do after their parents leave. I cried my eyes out after my parents left. My parents left the next day after my first class just to make sure everything ran smoothly. They were not happy about leaving me either. Everyone has to go through parental separation. I introduced myself and asked if she was also a freshman. To my luck, she was indeed a freshman.

She told me that her name was Megan Drummond. I always liked the name Megan. I noticed she had all kinds of country singer posters on her walls. I didn't like country music but differences are not important. We had a little difficulty understanding each other's speech. She spoke very slowly and softly. My speech can be slurred especially when I tense up when meeting someone new. However, it did not take long for us to understand each other almost perfectly. Later in our college career, we found out that our friends did not understand how we understood each other so well.

I could not figure out Megan's disability. The left side of her body looked fine, but the right side was paralyzed. I usually pride myself on being able to figure out people's disabilities by only looking at them. This comes from years of having friends and seeing people with physical disabilities. I thought she had cerebral palsy, but the characteristics did not all match. I did not want to ask her what her disability was right away, but I was curious.

After some small talk, I asked Megan if she would go to the dance with me. She became quiet. I hoped she would agree to go because she seemed kind. She also had a very good sense of humor. We started giggling right from the start. Little did we know this giggling habit would follow us throughout our lives. Megan smiled and agreed to go to the dance. I told her that I would stop by her room a little before the dance started and we could walk over to the University Center together. She looked relieved to meet someone too.

I went back to my room and continued to help my parents unpack. Unpacking took all day. I admit I felt proud that I asked Megan. I hoped we would get along. My parents were happy also. They wanted me to find good friends. They were a little scared leaving me at college. They hoped that I didn't get involved in drugs and alcohol. My dad gave me a lecture before I went to school. Falling in with a bad crowd was not in my agenda. I understood the temptations, but I was not going to mess up my life. I am the youngest child so it made it more difficult for my parents to let go.

I hoped that it was going to be that easy to make the rest of my friends. I wanted to remain outgoing so I said hi to people in the halls. I also remembered my assistant in high school telling me that if you have one good friend, you will be all right. So, I figured that I should at least be able to make one good friend.

Megan and I went to the dance together. Since it wasn't a formal dance, we wore shorts and T-shirts. The University Center was only across the street from Scranton. The air felt warm with soft breezes. I tried visualizing the mountains of snow and arctic air that everyone warned me about. I still could not believe I was in college. I actually made another of my goals. My next goal was to be a college graduate.

Megan and I did not talk much at first, but then we got on a roll. We kept making each other laugh. Apparently, we both enjoyed laughing and giggling. We always said it is better to laugh than cry. We found out that we had many similarities and differences. This combination, of course, has been the ongoing essence of our friendship.

Megan and I both graduated high school in June 1994. She lived two hours away from Edinboro in a town called Bradford. I lived six hours away in Spring City, a small suburb of Philadelphia. Our birthdays fell only a few days apart, but I am one year older. When Megan grew up, she did not have many opportunities to go out with friends. I had many friends. However, I considered them "in school" friends. Megan liked mainly country music. At that time, I hated country music. Over the years, thanks to Megan, I learned to appreciate country music. Megan also was not crazy about rock music, but she grew to like it because of me.

During the dance, Megan and I separated for a little bit. I wandered around the room and watched people dance. I tried to talk to some people, but the music blared making it difficult to hear each other. They held the dance in a big room called the Multipurpose room. This is where they hold all major university events or other activities. I did not meet anyone in particular. I do remember feeling a little hurt when I overheard a group of girls giggling and pointing at me. I heard one girl say, "I'm sure glad I'm not her." Sure, I know people are going to say mean things about what they do not fully understand. However, her words stung my ears and I never forgot them.

From what I had heard, mostly freshman went to the dance so they were probably just as shy as I was. Megan sat in the lobby watching people come in and out. One of Megan's favorite things to do is to people watch. People do very interesting things especially when they think no one is watching. I also noticed that Megan and I were the only ones that used wheelchairs at the dance. This surprised me because of the large population of students with disabilities.

After a while, the music annoyed us and the room became too crowded. I met Megan in the lobby. Megan and I decided to sit outside in front of the University Center since it was such a warm night. We discussed our families, school experiences and just our lives. Our families were similar by each having two siblings. I have an older brother and a sister. Megan has two brothers and she is in the middle. However, different from Megan's, my parents are divorced. We both had full time assistants to help us with our physical needs when we went to high school. We both wondered how we would survive without them.

As we continued talking, Megan and I discussed our disabilities. Luckily for us, Megan had total use of her left arm. Over the years, she took care of me whenever we went out to places. She fed me and helped as much as possible. She fed me better then some of my friends who can use both arms. I would help her too when I could. Some things took us awhile such as eating lunch at the mall, but we would do it. People would look at us funny, but that would just make us laugh. Things would have been much more difficult if Megan could not use her arm but knowing us, we would have managed.

When I began college, I had a boyfriend that lived back home. I told Megan a little about him. I missed him, but was exited about my new life. She told me that she never had a boyfriend or even went out on a date. Megan was very shy around boys and rarely talked to them. A good friend of hers in high school was a guy, but nothing romantic came from the friendship.

As we sat outside in the warm night air, Megan explained how shy she was. I was not an expert on men, but I have many close friends that were men. I decided to get Megan to make her first guy move in college. I knew she didn't want to walk back to the dorm alone, so I told her that I was not going to walk back to our dorm with her until she looked some guy in the eyes and said hello. Now that may sound cruel, but I knew Megan would feel a sense of accomplishment afterwards. I could also tell she wanted to do this but needed some persuasion. Friends have told me that I'm good at talking people into things. I can be very persuasive. I do not know whether this is a good thing or not.

We sat in front of the University Center for I do not know how long. I am guessing it was 20 minutes to a half an hour. I continued to insist that Megan complete this small task before we left. People must have thought that we were crazy. We were giggling as I pointed out men to whom she could say hello. Megan told me that she could not believe I was making her say hi to a guy. She did want to, though.

Finally, Megan looked up and stared her victim directly in the eyes. The man had dark hair and green eyes. She faintly said "Hi" to this guy and quickly put her head down. He said hello and entered the University Center. Either out of shock or fright, we both hit forward on our motorized wheelchairs and sped back to our dorm rooms laughing away. Megan felt extremely proud and happy she did that. I was also very proud of her and had an idea that this was going to be an interesting friendship.

Ever since that night, our friendship has grown and will hopefully continue to grow. The journey has not been all smooth and happy, but the important thing is that we made it. Megan and I argue, but somehow we manage to keep the friendship going. We completely understand the meaning of "Forgive and Forget."

Our sophomore year, I moved next door to Megan in room 17. The move was not deliberate. I planned on moving into room 18 because it was pink and had no tables fastened to the wall like 20 did. The tables made placing the carpet difficult. I didn't use the tables anyway.

As fate would have it, room 18 was under construction, so I decided on 17. That room also had no fastened tables, but was blue. I lived in 17 and Megan in room16 for the remaining years of college.

Living next door made seeing and communicating with each other easier. I would crawl from my room into hers instead of getting in and out of my chair. I did not do that often because, as you can imagine, it is not very good on your knees. I often wished that there were a door in the wall that connected our rooms. With a connecting door, I would not have to crawl down the hall. We would also tell each other good night by yelling through the wall and bang on the wall if one of our stereos were too loud.

When we visited each other, we would often speculate about our futures. We would discuss where we would live, whom would we marry and how we could keep our friendship going after graduation. Just when we thought we talked about everything, there seemed to be another topic that we didn't completely analyze.

Megan and I both went through our share of physical and mental changes during college. Megan grew her hair longer and now wears contact lenses. I cut my hair and grew it back again often. Our hair color changed a few times, and I got my ears pierced. Megan and I went through many fashion changes too. Although our sizes are different, we could borrow some tops from one another. Megan and I always asked for each other's advice no matter what the topic. We would not always follow the advice, but we would listen to it seriously.

Through the years, Megan and I learned to respect each other's opinion and listen to one another. This has not been all that easy but we did it. We also became leaders together in organizations and on our floor. Megan and I were in charge of the Organization for Disability Awareness for a year. This is a campus organization for disabled and non-disabled members. We do various activities on and around campus discussing important issues about disabilities. The women on our floor often took our advice. It made us both feel good that we could help others. We also have had lots of fun and plenty of laughter.

In the next chapter, Megan will talk about our freshman year. It was a year full of many changes and maturing for the both of us.

It was the best of times;
It was the worst of times...

by Megan

No, it's not *A Tale of Two Cities.* It's a tale of our freshman year. Freshman year is often the toughest time for students. They have to learn how to live on their own. Students must learn to deal with the increased amount of homework, and the fact that there is no one there to remind them every night to do that homework. There is also the social aspect of college life. Students have to learn to strike a balance between the social and the academic. Some do this successfully; others don't.

The first semester of college usually determines if a student is going to stay in school or go home and how they will do academically over the next fours years. It is very difficult to bring up a low grade point average, but it can be accomplished with a lot of work. This is often more true for a student with a disability. If they are used to having family members take care of their physical needs or help them with their homework, they may not adjust well when they have to ask strangers for help. The first year is truly a period of maturing and changing.

Edinboro University has a full-time staff of personal care attendants that are on the dormitory floor 24 hours a day. There is always someone around to assist a student with whatever they may need. Edinboro also provides academic aides for those students who need them. Academic aides help disabled students physically write their homework, put together projects and write out tests, but do not do the students' homework for them. They are the hands and the student with the disability gives direction.

After Jessica's parents left a few days after we moved in, Jessica and I started to hang out and call each other often. On the second night of school, Jessica called me because there was a cricket chirping in her room. I teased her about having a buggy room because we also found all kinds of spiders. Neither one of us had made a lot of friends at school yet either. We quickly became almost inseparable, even though we didn't have any of the same classes together. We ate lunch and dinner together and hung out in Jessica's room after we had finished our homework. We usually stayed in Jess's room because she is more comfortable sitting on the floor and I didn't have a carpet yet. We were constantly giggling at little jokes and life. The people on our floor took to calling us "the giggle twins" or "Frick and Frack" within the first few weeks.

The first weekend we were at school was Labor Day weekend. We both went home. Jessica flew, and my mom came to get me. Homesickness hit us harder than we thought it would. The next weekend, Jessica's boyfriend, Steve, and her brother, Christian, came up to visit her. So I went to check out the mall with some of the girls on the floor. The weekend after that, Steve and his friend came up to see her. I hung out with them some of the time, and also caught up on some studying. One of Jessica's friends was a big flirt and went crazy over Steve's friend. Her incessant flirting got on my nerves after a while so I left them alone.

The following weekend, we both went home again. Jessica already had plans to go to a Rolling Stones concert at Veterans Stadium in Philadelphia. She had never seen them in concert before. The Stones were not a band among my favorites, but I hoped she would have fun. I just wanted to go home because I was homesick.

We both went home often during our first semester. We were both homesick and had never really lived by ourselves before. Now we both wonder why we went home so often that semester. We should have enjoyed being at college and taken advantage of the resources and freedom available to us. Jessica went home more than I did in the spring of that year. She missed her boyfriend and family. I live a bit closer so my parents could visit more. That particular year my mom and dad were in Erie a lot so they came over to see me at school. I just didn't get to go home until spring break in March.

The first weekend Jessica and I were both up at school and no one came to visit, we decided to go to the mall. We went to the mall often during our college years. We had a good time and many experiences, but that's a whole different chapter.

After we had been at school for about a month, we started what we now refer to as our weekend tradition. If either of us had anything else to do or somewhere to go, we might miss a night. But we did the same thing almost every weekend until I graduated. We looked forward to the weekend especially when we had a lot of exams and projects. We could finally relax and catch up with each other.

The tradition took place in my room. Jessica would come over because I had a TV and VCR. At first, she stayed in her chair because she didn't feel like sitting on the hard floor. After I got a rug, we would both get down on the floor. I had gotten into the habit of taping *Friends* and *ER* so I could watch them over the weekend when I had time. Jessica liked them too. So, we would order dinner out somewhere and have it delivered. We would sit on the floor and eat dinner and watch TV or one of the movies I had brought with me. We also talked about anything and everything we could think of. Of course, Jessica and I spent a lot of time laughing and giggling too

We usually did this on Friday, Saturday and Sunday nights, unless we had something else to do. We would each take turns buying dinner and we would keep track of who bought when. On Sundays, we would order from the campus pizza place. Every student gets an account of $100 there, so they can order and it will just be taken off their account. We would also keep track of whose account we used when. Over the years, we learned to make our combined accounts last all year long with some leftover.

Even after I got a rug on my floor, we would sometimes decide to stay in our chairs to eat and watch TV. So I would feed Jessica. I'm pretty good at feeding her stuff like pizza or subs, which is what we normally ate. One night, though, she decided to try Buffalo Wings. I knew what they were but Jessica didn't. She wanted to try them, and I figured it wouldn't be that hard to feed them to her. I had forgotten that they are the kind of chicken wings that are smothered in gooey, sticky sauce. Her boyfriend had tried to feed her wings once and it didn't work that well. However, Jessica had forgotten what kind of wings Steve had tried to feed her and ordered them anyway.

We got them and started to eat. About halfway through the meal, I swore I would never again try to feed anyone but myself wings. We had sauce all over my room, my rug, Jessica's face and sweater, my jeans. Everywhere. I ruined that pair of jeans. The sauce stained them and I had to cut them off to make shorts. We laughed the whole time. After that, we decided to stick to pizza and subs. They're relatively safe.

The weather was another thing we adjusted too. Jessica lived in an area that had relatively mild winters compared to Edinboro. She thought that three inches of snow was a lot. I lived in the middle of a snow belt most of my life, so I knew what to expect. During the first snow, Jessica had to get used to maneuvering her wheelchair. I taught her a few things and she eventually grasped the technique. Driving a wheelchair through snow and ice isn't very fun. Fortunately, when Jessica's chair would get stuck another student would help her. My chair has bigger tires so I rarely got stuck.

On Valentine's Day, Jessica, our friends Grace and Diana and I ventured out to get Chinese food in town. Normally the trip would have taken ten minutes or less. On that particular Valentine's Day, though, the sidewalks were barely shoveled. It took us at least an hour. Grace, who did not use a wheelchair, exhausted herself pushing Jessica and Diana out of snow banks. The temperature was very low and the wind was not much help. I went ahead of the others in the hopes that I would get there in time to tell Jessica's academic aide that she was coming, but I was too late. By the time they got back to the dorm, I was warming up and they were frozen. After that, we all decided not try attempt to go into town when there was snow on the ground.

The first semester of that year went really smooth. Everything was so new to both of us. Our friendship was new too. We hardly had any problems. The few that we did have stemmed from her boyfriend and our *very* different personalities. She would tell me about some of their problems and ask for advice. Because I had a pretty strong feeling that the relationship would not last all through college and because I wanted to spare her the heartache of having it last years longer and then fall apart, the advice I gave usually included breaking up. Since Jessica did not want to do that, it caused a few minor tiffs.

The next semester, though, was a different story. Her relationship with Steve was getting rockier by the day, and I just couldn't keep my mouth shut when it came to what I considered to be mental and verbal abuse. Steve and Jessica were experiencing many difficult emotions, in part because of the distance between them. Steve would often say things just to be mean and hurtful to Jessica. This did not sit well with me. He did eventually let up doing this, and they were together until the summer before our senior year.

I told Jessica for weeks after that that they should break

up now, before she got hurt anymore. But she wasn't going to do that and we got into some bad fights about that. We fought about her and Steve, about who went home more often, about stupid stuff, really. We even fought over who was more feminine. Who knows what we were thinking when we came up with that one. It wasn't like we set out to argue, but this strange stuff would always pop out at us.

At the beginning of the spring semester, we both had a philosophy class with the same professor but at different times of the day. He did not want any disabled students in his class, and he made that quite clear. He told both of us point blank that he did not think either of us could do the work, even though he didn't know what either of us could do academically. He guaranteed Jessica a D in the class even if she did A work. He did not say this directly to me, but implied it every time we talked. Jessica chose to transfer into a different class and file a formal complaint against him. She did not want to endanger her GPA.

For some strange reason, that incident brought on a whole new set of arguments between us. I had chosen to stay in the class just to spite the professor. Anyone who knows me knows that that is just my nature. She thought this was kind of foolish because I was possibly going to hurt my grade point average. I passed with a C. I would have gotten a C in any philosophy class, not just that one. Philosophy is just not my forte.

We also had quite a few arguments because Jessica apparently thought I needed to change the way I was, and to some extent, still am. She thought I was suffering from depression because, unlike her, I did not want people around me all the time and because I was quiet and didn't say much around others. I would often just go into my room and not say a word to her or anyone else. This confused her because she thought I was upset with her or shutting her out. I didn't think, at the time, that it hurt her feelings. I just wanted to be alone and had never had to explain that to anyone before, so I didn't think to explain it to Jessica.

She would tell me at least once a week that I did not have to be the way I was. She wanted me to be happier and thought I couldn't be happy if I didn't constantly have someone around me. I told her that I would change when and if I wanted to and not until then. I also told her that I was not going to change because someone else thought I needed to. I had the attitude then, and still do, that if you don't like me the way I am then you don't have to be my friend. I explained to her that there were times when I just wanted to be alone. This was hard for her to understand at first, but she accepted it eventually and learned to leave me alone when I asked.

All of these fights took place before spring break in our freshman year. We both went our separate ways for break. She went home and made up with Steve for the umpteenth time. I went home and didn't really do a whole lot, but at least I wasn't in school. During break, we both had time to settle down and get everything in perspective. When we came back, we had a talk and settled everything. Jessica backed off about me changing who I was and I backed off about her and Steve breaking up, although I still thought the relationship would be over before we graduated. But I bit my tongue and kept quiet, which is very unlike me. I even helped her go through bridal magazines when she was feeling like he would propose.

Freshman year is difficult for any student. Getting adjusted to dorm life, making new friends, dealing with new responsibility. Freshman year was sad and great for Jessica and me. We learned a lot about each other, a lot about friendship, and a lot about life. Many things that we learned during our first year about communicating with each other, we apply today. Mostly, we learned when both of us really wanted advice or we just wanted someone to listen. Through all the fights and breakups and changes in each of us, our friendship survived. If it survived the beating it took that year, we are quite sure it can survive anything.

Jessica will now discuss how the Internet has influenced our friendship, other friendships, college and our lives.

Internet Friends
by Jessica

You might be wondering how the Internet could have an impact on our friendship and college life. Well, the answer is that the Internet had and continues to have a major impact on our friendship and experiences. In some ways, the Internet was both an advantage and a hindrance. The Internet became not only a source of entertainment and information, but also a great help for the survival of our friendship.

During the first semester and into the second semester of our freshman year, Megan and I did not realize all of the neat capabilities of our college Internet connection. The Internet was a fairly new development and neither of us used it very much. We had heard about the Internet, but not all of the details. We knew we could contact the school library, but that was about the extent of our knowledge. I used Prodigy since 1991 and used it at college to write email to my family and friends. I also met some good friends on it through the chat feature. Like many colleges today, every Edinboro University student receives an Internet account to do email and access the Internet. Students can do this either from their dorm room or any computer on and off campus. This makes college life easier.

If a student owns a personal computer and a modem,

they can reach the Internet in a dorm. I need to use a computer to write because my handwriting is illegible from cerebral palsy. Since I have to be on the floor when I type, I had a computer system complete with a modem placed within my reach. Obviously, getting down on the floor at a computer lab would be difficult and uncomfortable. Megan had a laptop computer and printer, but did not have a modem until the second semester.

Having our own computers made college easier. Megan and I could do our homework when we wanted and in the privacy of our own rooms. We did not have to trek all over campus to the labs. However, Edinboro has several computer labs around campus making it convenient for those who did not own computers. So, it is not a necessity to have a computer. Edinboro is also known for its extremely harsh winters. Snow and ice are not very fun to get around in especially when using a wheelchair. So, for us, having a computer made life much more convenient.

Just about every evening, after we finished our homework, Megan would come to my room. Megan and I would talk and listen to the stereo. We could easily talk for several hours about everything. Our conversations often drifted from pure silliness to complete seriousness. We would often debate very controversial issues such as abortion and gun control. Although these were heated topics, we would always seem to manage a compromise or a simple agreement to disagree. However, our debates changed our opinions on some topics. Other times, neither one of us had any idea what we were talking about. Sometimes, a woman who lived down the hall would yell at us for laughing too loud. Unfortunately, being yelled at would automatically make us laugh even more.

In the dorms, picking up radio stations was not easy. The antenna would have to be pointed in just the right position or forget it. Unfortunately, my stereo mainly picked up country stations, and I am not a big country fan. However, on one radio station I managed to tune in, they played only '70s music for an hour at night. Megan and I would listen and sing along with the music. We tried to keep our voices down as much as possible. However, at times we would get really involved. Both of us would pretend that we were natural born singers.

Toward the beginning of our second semester, a mutual friend of ours introduced us to a new world. Kane worked as a meal aid at the cafeteria. He was also a freshman. Meal aides helped the students with disabilities. They help get the student's food and feed them if they need to be fed. I need to be fed or I tend to make a mess. Kane often fed me lunch and dinner whenever he worked. Megan and I would always try to eat meals together. Sometimes our schedules would conflict but most of the time we could manage at least one meal together. Kane had a very unique sense of humor and made Megan and I laugh.

One evening at dinner, Kane talked about how to use Telnet using our Internet connection. With Telnet, someone can connect to many other computers nearly all over the world. At first, Megan and I were not too impressed, but then he explained further. We were not too technically advanced. Kane explained how we could connect to a computer and chat to many people all at once. We could chat to all kinds of people from all over the world. Now Megan and I were hooked and were ready to enter the world of cyberspace. When it came to talking to people, Megan and I were experts.

Kane came over to my room a couple of nights later. He showed me how to connect to something called the Resort through Telnet on my computer. Connecting to the Resort was easier than I imagined. I just had to get to the Telnet prompt and then type the address and I was there – the cyberresort. After connecting, the whole system was a bit overwhelming. At first, all you see are all these people talking at once. Kane taught me how you can talk to one person or an entire room at a time. I got the hang of chatting quickly.

To be considered a Resort resident, you need to have a few things. You must have a screen name, valid email address and password. For the first year, I chose MsJess as my screen name. I changed it to Jessica about a year later when it became available and because I am not one for nicknames. I was amazed that this connection was even possible and free. When I was fifteen, I had a similar system on my Commodore that made it possible to talk to many people online. However, you had to pay by the minute to use it and that got me into serious trouble. I became easily addicted and that added up to many minutes and much money. So, this whole Resort notion simply amazed and thrilled me.

When Megan got a modem, I quickly taught her how to connect and use the Resort. She was as excited as I was to use it. Megan fell in love with the Resort almost immediately. She liked meeting new people and chatting. She had never seen anything like it before. Megan used a childhood nickname as her screen name because someone was already using the name Megan. A year later, Megan changed her screen name to a combination of her first and middle names. She liked that name a lot better. Unfortunately, a hacker had tampered with Megan's Resort account and she had to erase the earlier screen name anyway.

The Internet opened new opportunities for us. The people on the Resort could not judge us by our physical disability. No one can see our disabilities over the computer. Whoever said that the Internet was the great equalizer knew what they were talking about. People can only see what you type unless you are into those Internet cameras, but neither Megan nor I are into that just yet. It is up to you to decide how much you want someone to know about you. Megan and I told people about our disabilities and they had different reactions. Some accepted us completely, but others did not want anything to do with us. These are normal reactions in society as well. Of course, not giving too much personal information is wise because you do not know who exactly is on the other side. Mostly college students and people around our age use the Resort. The people that we meet do not treat us any differently than anyone else because our disabilities are hidden.

Megan and I not only met new people on the Resort, but we talked to each other as well. Our friends in the dorm would often tease us because they would usually hear us say, "See you on the computer!" Everyone got a big kick out of it. We lived right next door to each other but we used the Internet for communication. Chatting is that much fun to do! It would annoy my family and my other friends because my phone line would be constantly busy at night. Sometimes they would write me email just so they could call me.

We talked through the Internet for various reasons besides it being fun. Besides classes, Megan and I were usually together. We would either be in my room, her room, the cafeteria, outside, the mall, but no matter where we were, we would be together. However, there were times during the day that we did our own thing. We had other friends to see and meetings to attend. No one should be with each other 24 hours a day. After we would get ready for bed, we often stayed in our own rooms. We did homework, read, listened to the stereo, watched television or called people. Every night, at the usual time, we would get on the Internet, write email and chat to each other as we talked with others.

Megan and I discussed professors, our homework, friends and just caught up on things. We felt comfortable in our own rooms especially on those blustery winter nights. We did not have to go anywhere. Neither Megan nor I were really into drinking or going out on weeknights. In fact, we did not do much of that during the weekends. We did go out, but partying was not our main priority. When we became tired of the Internet, we could just hop into our beds and go to sleep.

Another reason Megan and I used the Internet was to clear up any unsettled business that we had between us during the day. We still use the Internet for this reason.

Although Megan and I are best friends, we do have our share of disagreements and conflicting personalities. After all, people cannot agree on everything, even best friends. A few of these arguments became very nasty and almost ended our friendship all together. Luckily, the friendship is still going strong. We learned, however, that when we were face to face we often became carried away and more emotional. I've been told that I can be over emotional at times, and I suppose that is true. Instead of dealing with the issues, we would end up accidentally, and sometimes purposefully, hurting each other's feelings. Sticking to the issue is obviously the best solution for dealing with arguments.

Megan and I then started to use the Internet to discuss our feelings and sort our differences out. We would either write email about our feelings to one another or get on the Resort and discuss the problem. Usually, we found that being open with the written word was easier than talking about it. We could also express ourselves a lot better by writing. Megan and I usually followed up major arguments with a face to face conversation, but it was less threatening and easier to do. Using the Internet in this way has helped our friendship tremendously.

The negative side to the Internet dealt with our grades. If you use the Internet, you know how addicting it can be. Megan and I would tend to procrastinate from doing our work especially as we entered our senior year. We would sign on to the Resort and begin chatting away and lose track of time. Megan and I needed to keep a balance between schoolwork and chatting. We would often tease each other that we would be 4.0 students if it were not for the Internet. I guess we will never know.

Currently, Megan and I are still using the Internet. In fact, we use it now more than ever. Since graduation, Megan and I do not have the opportunity to see each other every day anymore. We live six hours away from each other, so our friendship relies heavily on the Internet, the Resort and email. Megan and I meet every night around the same time and chat. We chat with mutual friends also on the Internet. Instead of using the Resort, we now use AOL Instant Messenger (AIM.) AIM is a common chat program used on the Internet and it is easier than the Resort.

We also email each other at least two or three times a week. Megan and I also call each other once a week, alternating weeks. However, jamming a week's worth of happenings into a once-a-week 45-minute phone call is quite difficult. Especially because we are both busy and have a lot to tell each other. The Internet has certainly made our friendship so much easier and closer.

Other than using the Internet as a way of communicating with each other, Megan and I have found new friends, enhanced our careers and found a lot of valuable information. We both built web pages for ourselves and after I graduated, I learned more about designing web pages. I decided to try my hand in my own business designing web pages. I took a class in business over the summer. Megan allowed me to design her web page in which she posts her writings and other information about herself. I have a personal and business web site. I now create web sites for businesses and people. I will probably continue doing so until I become too occupied with teaching and a family of my own.

Megan and I write articles for web sites. This has given us an opportunity to work together even though we are so far apart. I also volunteer at a search engine editing and reviewing web sites. I teach and take courses online as well.

Our mall adventures were very interesting and moments we will never forget. They could fill a whole book, but they only fill a chapter here.

Scenes From A Mall
by Megan

Jessica and I spent a lot of time at the Millcreek Mall in Erie over the four years we were in school together. Probably too much time, but we had a lot of fun. The mall is about a 45-minute bus ride from campus and the bus usually left around 10:30 in the morning. Going to the mall was also a way of escape from the campus for a few hours. We are definitely women that like to shop. There is also not a whole lot of other stuff to do in Edinboro on a Saturday afternoon, especially if you can't drive and have to walk everywhere.

We learned about this lack of activity in Edinboro about a month and a half into the first semester. After everyone had been up to visit Jessica on the weekends and we had both been home a couple of times, we spent our first Saturday afternoon in the dorms. The dorms are virtually deserted on the weekends. It is very quiet and there is little to do but homework. Doing homework is good, but we needed some fun things to do too.

The next Saturday, Jessica and I decided that we would try the mall. We were just looking to get off campus and be around people. Riding the city bus that went to the mall was always an exciting adventure. When we first started going, the drivers did not always secure the wheelchairs. They must have figured our chairs were stable enough that they wouldn't move during the trip. The buses were also only equipped to handle four chairs at a time, but the drivers would try to pack in as many as they could. There were sometimes eight to 10 chairs on the bus. We felt like a pack of sardines. This form of transportation is very unsafe and a lot of people complained, but nothing ever got done. If you didn't like it, then you could just stay in the vacant dorm.

Jessica and I made it on the bus and survived the trip. When we got into the mall for the first time, we were lost. Neither one of us knew our way around. The newness made exploring exciting. The mall is not too big, but not very small either. We explored every store and spent money like we had never bought anything before. We had a great time. Now we know the mall like the back of our hands.

After we had wandered around a while, our stomachs reminded us that we needed to eat. We found a McDonalds. Since we hadn't found any of the restaurants in the mall yet, we decided to eat there. After lunch, though, we decided that we weren't going to go back there again. There are only two accessible tables in the place. A young couple with a baby was at one, and a man sitting by himself, not even eating, was at the other one. Jessica and I were not impressed. Neither person would move, and when we asked an employee to ask them to move, the worker said that they had just as much right to sit there as we did.

Jessica and I sat outside the window and waited for one of them to move so that we could get the table before someone else sat down. We waited about an hour and finally got to a table. We were too hungry and stubborn to go find another place. I took Jessica's money and order while she stayed at the table. When our lunch was ready, the counterperson handed me the tray and walked away. Since I can only use one arm, obviously I couldn't drive and carry the tray. I sat in front of the counter for at least 10 minutes before someone offered to take the tray. A little girl carried the tray for me instead of an employee.

We both ordered Chicken McNuggets because we figured that would be the easiest thing to feed Jessica. She got honey dipping sauce for hers and I got barbecue sauce. At the time, I had never opened one of those little packages so I wasn't very good at it. I tried it and the package slipped out of my hand. There was honey everywhere. It was all over my jeans, the front of Jess's overalls, our table. We thought it was quite amusing, but the people around us just looked at us with disgust. We didn't allow them to ruin our mood. They looked at us with even more disgust when I started to feed Jessica her McNuggets. I guess they weren't used to seeing people eat lunch. Disabled people, at any rate.

After we had finished and cleaned up all of the honey that we could, we left our tray on the table and left the restaurant. The table we were at was at the back, near the entrance to the restrooms. I backed my chair up and turned around to follow Jessica through the crowd and outside. Just as I started to go forward, a man who wasn't paying attention to where he was going ran into me and dumped the remainder of his lunch on my lap. I apologized, even though I wasn't at fault, and brushed off my lap. While I did, the guy stood there and yelled, loud enough for most of the place to hear, what a stupid idiot I was and that people like me shouldn't be allowed out in public. I thought he was going to hit some old man who pointed out that it wasn't my fault. Anyway, that's why we decided to quit going to McDonalds

The next time we went, which was the next weekend I think, we found a Burger King. That was a whole different atmosphere. They had two accessible tables that were reserved for the disabled, and the employees usually enforced that whoever was sitting there had to move if a disabled customer needed one of the tables. I usually did the ordering while Jessica saved the table. The counter help there would carry our tray to the table automatically. I wouldn't even have to ask. And when Jessica order a fountain drink that I couldn't get, the same person who carried our tray would get it for her. We were always going to write a letter to that Burger King's manager and tell her what a good job the staff did, but we never got around to it.

We had a few interesting experiences at Burger King. One Saturday, we were sitting in the back dining room because the accessible tables were both being used. We were eating and talking, not bothering anyone, when an old lady came over to our table. I don't even remember her name now, but her granddaughter's name was Jen and she was an art major at Edinboro. She had seen the Edinboro jacket that Jessica was wearing and the sweatshirt that I was wearing and thought we might know her. Then she started in on how great of an accomplishment it was that Jessica and I were going to college. We just smiled and nodded and tried not to giggle. We couldn't help giggling, though, when she started to tell us about her arthritis. We had no idea why this woman told us her life story. She thought we were just happy college girls out on a Saturday. Before we really started laughing, she saw her son and had to leave. It was an odd conversation, but we know she was just trying to be friendly.

After we ate lunch, there was nothing left to do but shop and hang out. The first couple of years, we could spend the whole time until the bus came at 3:30 just looking through the stores. By the time the last semester of my senior year rolled around, we could go into the mall, look in almost every store, get what we needed and be ready to leave by about 2:00. We knew the mall in and out so the newness of going ran out. We both wished we could drive so we could leave when we were finished. Unfortunately, we were left to wait for the bus and that is when we took up people watching.

We would sit at the edge of the main promenade, where the entrances are, and just watch people come in and go out. We would usually split a Coke or a small bag of cookies from the Original Cookie Company. Other times we would just watch people. Sometimes, Jessica and I would count people in a certain category. We counted the number of people coming in wearing red jackets or the number of people going out with baby carriages. We would count to a certain number and then usually give up. Many times, though, we would just wonder about people. One afternoon while we were sitting there, a man in his late 20s or early 30s must have come in and gone out at least 15 times in the span of 45 minutes. Jessica and I figured that he was lapping the mall, but we couldn't come up with a reason why. Perhaps it was his weekly exercise routine since the weather was so cold. Most of the time we just sat there and talked. We talked about relationships, college events, our futures and families. The idea for this book was born sitting in the mall one afternoon.

We only seemed to run into one or two really bizarre mall occurrences a year. The parent of a small child literally grabbing the child to get him out of the path of what the parent obviously considered a dangerous threat, i. e. our wheelchairs, seemed a bit bizarre at first, but it became pretty commonplace. Parents would also snap at their children and tell them not to bother us when the child tried to ask a question. That also became a commonplace occurrence at the mall. We aren't out to run little children over. We both love children and encouraged questions.

One day in our freshman year, Jessica and I went to the mall with our friend Diana. There is a bench right inside the doors. After we all got through the doors, we stopped to have a little conference and decide what we were going to do first. There was a small group of older people sitting on the bench. I can't figure out why seeing three women in wheelchairs would frighten anyone, but obviously it did. They all got up and moved as far away from us as they could, all looking as if they were scared to death. When we passed them later in the day, they again hurried to the opposite side from where we were. We just giggled and let it go.

Jessica and I noticed they had Glamour Shots at the mall, in our sophomore year. We often discussed going and getting our pictures done. Jessica thought it would be a great present for her boyfriend for Valentine's Day. We talked to a woman that worked there and she said that we could get glamorized and pictures taken for ten dollars. The next question was who were we going to ask to help us change outfits when we did the pictures. Jessica asked her friend, Grace, to help her. I asked our friend Alyson. The next week was our appointment. We all took the bus to the mall and got to the place on time. We picked outfits. We both picked sexy outfits as well as conservative looks. Then came the makeup and hair. Grace and Jessica were directing the women on how to do the hair and so on. They thought the outfits I picked out were too conservative and boring, so Jess and Grace picked out my clothes for the shoot. We figured that we might as well look our best.

After we were all made up, it was time for pictures. I went first. Luckily during the shoot Grace noticed that out in the mall there was a television monitor showing the whole mall my photo shoot, without my permission. She told them to shut it off and stood in front of the monitor to try and block it. During the change of outfits, all you wear is a tank top. Nothing that we really needed to show the public. Jessica went next. Grace, Alyson and I all sat in the doorway trying to make her laugh. She relaxes more and her smiles come out really nice.

When all the pictures were shot, we could decide what ones we wanted. They were on a computer and we could pick them. It came out to be on the expensive side, but we had lots of fun and our families and friends liked the pictures.

Another time at the mall, Jessica decided to get her ears pierced. I have had my ears pierced most of my life. I supported Jessica's decision and went with her. We were both apprehensive because her cerebral palsy causes involuntary movements especially when she is nervous and tries to sit still. Jessica kept on asking me how bad it hurt and I assured her that she would be fine. Jessica told the women at the piercing place that it might be a good idea if someone held her head still as the other pierced. I sat next to her and all went well. In less than five minutes, Jessica had her ears pierced with little discomfort.

The rest of freshman year at the mall was relatively uneventful. The next year, though, I went to the mall one day when Jessica had gone home for the weekend so I could buy her Christmas present. I must have looked lonely or out of my element because everyone felt compelled to talk to me or tell me what they had bought or were going to buy. I decided to go and sit in McDonalds where there were people around after some man, well-intentioned but a little scary, followed me around trying to show me the baby gerbil he had bought for his girlfriend. He meant well, but it was a little freaky.

In our junior year, Jessica and I were in the mall looking at dresses that I might want to wear to our sorority formal. We had already been stopped a few times by friends of ours or people we knew somehow, so we didn't think anything about it when were heard someone call and ask us to wait a minute. We thought it was just one of our friends. An older woman who neither of us recognized came up to us. We were polite and friendly and asked her what we could do for her. She pointed at me and asked where I had gotten my "cart." She said her husband had recently suffered a stroke and could use one to get around. It took me a minute to realize that she was talking about my wheelchair. Jessica knew right away what she was talking about because she'd had people ask that of her before. She rattled of something while I was trying not to laugh. Finally, I told her that I had gotten my chair through a vendor in DuBois and not anywhere in the area. She looked heartbroken when I told her I wasn't sure where she could get a chair for her husband, but she thanked us and went on her way.

Jessica's sister, Hannah, visited Jessica a few times at college. One time, we went to the mall on a Saturday afternoon. We wandered around the mall like always. But then we passed by the pet store. Jessica and I never go in because it is usually crowded and she hates seeing the puppies in cages. She is a big dog lover. Anyway, Hannah convinced us to go in the store. We looked at a few dogs and then we were ready to leave, but then a Dalmatian puppy caught Hannah's eye. Hannah and Jessica had a Dalmatian at home so they felt compelled to look at the puppy. Then Hannah got the idea in her head to hold the puppy. Jessica and I protested because we knew that when she held the puppy, she would be hooked.

Jessica and I were correct. Hannah bonded with the puppy and wanted to buy it. She had her own apartment and could take care of it. We all wandered around the mall discussing the pros and cons of buying her. Hannah finally decided to buy her but when we went back to the store, the clerk said the puppy had been sold five minutes earlier. We felt disappointed but then thought that maybe it was for the best.

The next day when Hannah and Jessica walked back from the dining hall, they saw the woman who worked at the pet store. Apparently, she worked at the pet store and was a student at Edinboro. She told us that the man that was going to buy the puppy never did and she was still on sale. She said that she would even take Hannah to the mall to buy her. Hannah said yes and bought the puppy who is now a very active three-year old dog named Annabelle. When Hannah came back to the dorm with the puppy, people kept coming in and out just to see her. Like all puppies, she liked to bite so we were all thankful when she fell asleep. Monday morning Hannah and Anna went home and now Anna has a sister, another Dalmatian named Duchess.

The last year that Jessica and I went to the mall together was pretty uneventful. By the beginning of my last semester, we wanted something else to do on Saturdays. That's when we figured out that we could make a transfer at the mall and go to Tinseltown, a theater/restaurant/arcade a few miles up the road from the mall. We only went a few times, but because of the way the buses ran, we could see two movies every time. It was relatively cheap as well. We could get four tickets, two pieces of pizza or two hot dogs, and two sodas for $24.

We would get back to the mall from Tinseltown at about 5:30 and the bus back to campus didn't come until 6:30. We would get back to the mall and go to one of the music stores because, inevitably, one or both of us would want the music from one of the movies we had just seen. After we got our CDs, we would take our usual spots by the entrance and wait for the bus.

Usually, at the time of the afternoon, a lot of the people who felt compelled to talk to us had gone home. There was a day, though, that one older lady who took the bus back to Edinboro with us cornered Jessica into a conversation. We had just seen the re-release of *Grease*. Apparently this woman was a John Travolta fan because she talked to Jess about him for at least 15 minutes. Then she wanted to know our majors and how we were doing in school and what our disabilities were. We both know that she was just being friendly, but we were glad when the bus came or we would have ended up telling her our life stories.

That was one of the last times we went to the mall together. After I graduated, Jessica went sometimes with other friends. I visited Jessica for the weekend and we went to the mall on Saturday. No old people ran away from us and no parents scolded the children for bothering us. Our waitress at Ruby Tuesday was very friendly and didn't even stumble at the sight of seeing two disabled people eating lunch together. It was a pretty quiet day at the mall, especially for Jessica and me.

Jessica visited her friend, Alyson, a semester after graduation. I asked my mom to take me up to the mall so I could see Jessica and do some shopping. Jessica did not have her motorized chair so it made it slightly difficult to talk, but we were able to talk when we ate. Nothing strange happened that time either, but it was nice to see each other again.

The mall will always be the same no matter where you are. There will always be protective parents, strange people, friendly people and rude people. Jessica and I have already learned to deal with them. Now they need to learn to deal with us.

Sorority Days
by Jessica

To many college students, joining a sorority or fraternity is very important and the highlight to the college experience. To some, pledging is as crucial as obtaining a degree. For the first two years of college, I thought sororities and fraternities were nothing but a big waste of time and money. I also felt that I did not have time to pledge with my courses and other obligations. To me, sororities seemed as if they just wanted women to buy their friends and to all dress the same. I felt that I was an individual and did not want to go down that route.

Whenever we discussed sororities, Megan felt that sororities were a waste of time as well as a waste of money. However, she was also a little more interested in joining one than me. She saw herself in a sorority, but did not know what one to join. Megan had also wanted someone to join along with her.

The formal aspect of a sorority, however, did interest the two of us. A sorority formal is a fancy dance toward the end of each semester. The purpose of a formal is to welcome in the new members and give out awards officially. A formal is also exciting and fun. It gives a good reason to dress up. I liked going and dressing up for the prom so I figured I would like going to a formal. That reasoning sounds very superficial now, but at the time my reasoning made sense.

In my freshman year, I asked around about sororities. My interest grew because I began to meet more people that belonged to one. Some sorority sisters asked my friend, Grace, and me to join a service sorority the spring of that year. We both thought it over, but decided that we were too individualistic and did not join. We also had a lot of schoolwork and projects to do. To us, academic work was more important. The thought of joining never left my mind though. My interest grew from just the formal. Now I wanted to meet people and do different activities as a group.

When our junior year came, I already belonged to a national service fraternity for special education. We did activities and service projects for children with special needs. I liked it and the urge to join a sorority hit me frequently. I just needed an extra push to get me to join. I am not exactly sure what changed my mind. I guess peer pressure and just some need to belong to something like that. I was not the only one that felt the same way. Megan was going through the same feelings but we never discussed it.

Then one day, Megan mentioned that she was thinking about joining a service sorority. I was a little surprised because I did not realize that she wanted to do it. I thought about how fun it would be to join with Megan. I did feel apprehensive that Megan might feel as if I was taking her idea. That was not so at all. It was just that I was thinking about joining anyway. I wrote Megan email about it. Unfortunately, my thoughts and fears came true. Megan thought I was doing it because of her and that was only some of my reasoning for joining.

Megan and I were also having problems other than just the sorority. Steve and I were having problems with our relationship. We had constant problems ever since I started college and looking back on it, I should have broken the relationship off before college. I was upset this particular morning about some disagreement we had. I was quiet about it in the morning with Megan because I did not want to get all upset before class. So, I decided to keep quiet until I was finished with classes. Megan and I were taking Oceanography together that semester, a course that we both barely passed. We had this class at 10 o'clock that morning. My friend, Grace, was in the class and asked me why I looked so sad.

Then all my feelings came out and before I knew it, I told her what happened with Steve. I did not mean to but it just all came out. By telling Grace first, I hurt Megan. In the dorm, Megan was quieter than usual and I tried to explain what had happened. I did not mean to hurt her, but I did. She was not very happy with me. I did not want to argue so I wished her a good weekend because she was going home. I went back to my room and wrote her email and explained everything the best I could to her. Before Megan went home, she wrote me and she understood my feelings but she also wrote that Steve and I could both do better.

Being sensitive at the time, that comment hurt me a lot. I felt hurt because Megan did not seem to hold a high regard for me if she thought Steve could do better than me. It made me wonder what kind of person she really thought I was. Usually, it does not bother me too much what people think of me, but it really matters if it is someone I care about. In this case that person was my best friend.

When Megan got back from her weekend at home, we fought this out through the telephone, face to face, on the Internet and email. It was quite the ordeal to say the least. We were both too stubborn to listen to one another. Megan thought I did not value her opinion by not coming to her first. I thought Megan thought I was a horrible girlfriend to Steve and creating all of our problems.

The night came that the women interested in joining the sorority became pledges. A pledge is not yet a sister, but working her way to become a full member of the sorority. Megan and I were still arguing and trying to sort our problems out. We had been arguing for about a week and it was getting the best of us. We are normally happy and laugh a lot. We turned into very sad women who almost forgot to smile. A lot of our friends began to worry, but they knew we would sort things through.

The entire first floor quickly knew of our argument. As in many college dorms, news spreads very quickly and many exaggerations get added into it. Our misery became the floor's gossip happy hour. However, some of our really good friends tried to help us get over it. I think they missed our friendship too. The night came when we had to leave to go to the meeting. Then Megan and I had to see each other and be in the same room together for a few hours. I felt nervous to see her but also relieved. I missed her so much but I was still very hurt.

Megan and I ran into each other in the hallway before the meeting. Megan's eyes were red and puffy. We both knew we missed each other, but both of us were too stubborn to apologize first. Then the biggest argument we ever had started. We started to argue in Megan's room, but then it was getting late. A friend of ours offered to walk with us to the meeting. She probably regretted that decision. She walked in front of us with Megan and me trailing behind yelling at one another. We did apologize to her afterwards and she understood our situation.

Megan and I stopped arguing as we waited for the elevator. We both finally understood that we wanted our friendship back. We started giggling at how ridiculous we were for letting our argument get so out of hand. Before entering the room, the start of our sisterhood, we agreed to sort our problem out and work out our friendship. Megan and I did sort things out slowly, but we did it. That night, we were also inducted as pledge sisters.

At first, the sorority was fun. A pledge receives a big sister. A big sister is someone who has already been in the sorority. She becomes your mentor and helps you out. They know all the incoming sisters as pledges. A pledge decorates her door, carries a pledge book, wears a pin and goes to meetings. The main purpose of this sorority is to do service. The other purpose was to meet new people, get to know the other sisters and work as a group. When you volunteer, it can be any kind of volunteer service, but you need some proof that you completed the work. You can do this alone or with the entire sorority. Sometimes you had no choice and had to do service projects with the entire group even on snowy Saturday mornings.

The sorority held meetings once a week and they could last up to three hours. The meetings would begin around

8:30 or 9 at night. Now it would not have been bad if it was a productive three hours, but for the most part it was more complaining. Megan and I are not really like that. We liked to get work done and not sit around and talk about it. Our lack of interest in meetings was our first clue that perhaps sorority life was just not for us. The other pledges were also much more excited and much more willing to conform to sorority standards than we were.

The pledge period did have its good points. We volunteered to help the campus and other good causes. We met some interesting people and participated in activities that we would have never otherwise considered. Our families were happy we joined, however, our grades suffered some. They did not suffer too terribly, though, because we knew our grades were far more important than a sorority.

After the pledge period completion, which was now the beginning of November, there was an induction ceremony at a church in Edinboro. The night of the ceremony, the weather was absolutely miserable. It was very cold, snowy and icy. Megan and I wanted to stay in the dorm because it was so miserable outside. The other pledges and sisters were truly excited to go to the ceremony no matter the weather. Megan and I even tried to get out of going, but we could not. We also knew that it was a dress occasion. However, we did not go all out like most of the women did. We wore jeans and nice sweaters. Almost everyone else wore dresses and skirts. We did feel slightly out of place, but at that time all of the sisters knew our hearts were not completely into the sorority.

Finally, we officially were members of the sorority. We were sure that the other sisters hated us because we were definitely not the typical sorority stereotypes. As a new sister, you have certain responsibilities. A big one is to make a paddle for your big sister and white rose sister. In return, they make you a photo album and a pillow. A paddle is a piece of wood with the sorority's Greek letters and other symbols concerning the sorority, including the theme of that particular pledge class, painted on it. Luckily, another sister of ours offered to make our paddles for us. We just had to tell her where we wanted everything placed.

After she made the paddles, we could sit back and enjoy the formal. We were both excited and looking forward to the formal. I asked my fiancé at the time to go with me. Steve reluctantly agreed to drive six hours during the winter for the formal. However, Megan needed to find a date. She was not dating anyone nor did she have any guy friends that would attend a formal with her. She definitely did not want to go alone.

I discussed Megan's dilemma with my friend, Grace. She did personal care work for a guy who lived off campus. He had a roommate, Aaron, that Grace thought might be interested in going to the formal with Megan. Grace asked him and sure enough he said he would like to go. Megan felt relieved, but nervous to go on a blind date. I assured Megan that it was only one night and Steve and I would be right there with her. Aaron and Megan did meet a few days before the formal so it was not too awkward. They also seemed to like each other so that was definitely a good sign.

Unfortunately, Megan had another problem. Megan's wisdom teeth came in and hurt her like crazy. Due to her schedule, she could not leave college to get them pulled. So, she had to suffer through the pain until Thanksgiving break. Luckily, that was only a few days after the formal. Megan could hardly eat anything. She mainly ate French fries, ice cream and milkshakes. She was hungry, but she could not chew anything solid. I felt bad because I had my wisdom teeth out the summer before and knew how badly it hurt.

Despite Megan's pain, she decided to go to the formal. Excitement filled the air on the night of the formal. A few other women that lived on our floor were also sorority sisters and were going to the formal. Megan and I arranged for our friends to help us get ready. The personal care workers that worked the normal shift helped us get dressed. We had friends come over and help with our hair and make up. Megan's mom was in Edinboro for her brother's basketball game that day so she came to help her and see her all dressed up. Megan made her leave before her date came so he would not be too intimidated. Megan wore a black velvet dress, and I wore a dark green velvet dress. As our friends made us up, Megan and I giggled and chatted away about what was in store that night.

Megan and I looked at the clock every few minutes. She was nervous and so was I even though I knew Steve for years. Aaron and Steve arrived on time. Steve wore a dark green suit and looked handsome. Aaron wore a gray suit and Megan especially liked his Drakkar cologne. Megan and I giggled a lot like we so often do. We felt excited and happy that we were in the organization even though we did not quite fit in. Our friends took pictures for us. Aaron got on his knee to be at the same level as Megan. At the time, it seemed like a good idea, but in the pictures he appeared to be three feet tall. After the pictures were taken, our friends wished us a good time. Then we were off for our first sorority formal.

The Office for Students with Disabilities van took us to the formal because neither Megan nor I owned our own van. Aaron drove to the formal and met us there. Megan was not too impressed by that. She hoped that he would ride with the three of us. When we arrived, we had some difficulty getting into the place. During the week we had had some terrible snowstorms and snow and ice were everywhere. Steve assisted Megan and me through the snow. We joined Aaron at the entrance. We waited in the lobby as the staff prepared the formal room. Everyone looked so dressed up and nice. I hardly recognized some of my friends, and they hardly recognized us.

As the saying goes, time flies when you're having fun. After we were seated in the crowded room, we ate dinner. Megan and I were placed at two different tables, but we switched seats with a couple so we were not separated. Dinner was buffet style so everyone could choose what he or she wanted to eat. Megan could not chew yet because of her teeth. The worst part of it was that she was starving. She dined on dinner rolls and anything soft that she liked. Aaron and Steve did not hit it off very well. They had different very personalities and interests. So, Megan and Aaron were in their little conversation and Steve and I were in ours.

Since we had a big pledge class, the ceremony took a really long time. We were in a small and cramped room. That made things uncomfortable. Each sister had to present her gift to the other sister and that felt like it took forever. Everyone was bored during that part of the ceremony. People kept on getting up to get drinks or get fresh air. The ceremony was the longest period that night.

After all the presentations, about 45 minutes later, people started to dance. We were happy to move finally. The disc jockey had a few too many drinks so he was really funny. He was making everyone laugh by his jokes and acting all goofy. Due to the small dance floor, some people started to dance on the tables. Steve and I did not dance at all. Steve is not into dancing. I like to dance so Megan and I went to the dance floor. We only danced one song and it was even too crowded and extremely hot for us to have a good time.

Around 11:00, Steve and I were tired and he had to drive home the next day. The van had arrived to take us back to the dorms and we were ready. Unfortunately, Aaron had just asked Megan to dance with him. I did not know that, but Megan did agree to leave. Later she told me that he asked her and I felt bad she did not have an opportunity to dance with him. If I had known, I would have waited until after they danced.

So, it was time to find our coats. A big problem was about to unfold. Megan's mom let her borrow her leather jacket. The jacket was very nice and meant a lot to her mother. Well, no one could find her coat when it was time to go. Megan panicked. She felt horrible about losing her mom's coat. We checked everywhere. Megan wore Aaron's suit jacket home and tried to think of a way to tell her mom she lost her jacket. Fortunately, her dad knew the owners of the place and they were able to find the coat for her. Aaron said he would pick up the jacket if anyone there found it.

Aaron and Steve helped get Megan and me back on the van. Later that week, the place did find the jacket and Aaron picked it up for her. Their friendship did continue for a little bit, but nothing serious came from it.

We were full-fledged sisters the second semester of our junior year. The gap grew wider and wider between the other sisters and us. We tried to be friends with the sisters, but we had nothing in common. A few of them we were friends with, but none that we were close to. For me, doing service projects was the highlight of the sorority. Much of what Megan and I did not like was how the sisters claimed to love each other yet all you heard were nasty rumors about other people and constant complaining.

A person talking behind other people's backs is one thing I really cannot stand. This especially bothers me when they claim to be friends with the person. I always try to defend the other person no matter who it may be. I know I would not appreciate it if someone were talking behind my back. Megan and I did not want to become wrapped up in the name-calling and constant complaining. So, we kept to ourselves during the meetings and service projects. We both felt that we just did not belong. We were very academic-oriented as well and many of the sisters were not.

Before we knew it, the spring formal was only a couple of weeks away. The semester seemed to fly by. The longer we were in college, the faster time went. I again asked Steve to go to the formal with me. He agreed and I wore a dress that I bought during Christmas break. I know it was early, but the dress was very pretty and at a great price. The dress was antique white, long, and lacy. Megan brought a dress, but she decided not to wear it because it was not appropriate for a formal. The dress was electric blue and more for a club or a semi-formal event. Our friend, Erin, let her borrow her mom's dress. It was a deep red and looked very attractive on Megan.

Megan again needed to find a date to go with her. Time was beginning to run out. The formal was in the end of April. Aaron was out of the picture. She asked Kane, who was a meal aid, to go. He turned her down nicely because dances are not really his thing. He said it was nothing personal, and he really did mean it. We were quickly running out of options. Megan and I spent hours talking about who would be available to go.

One night, we were having dinner with our friend Alyson. Megan told Alyson her dilemma. Alyson thought about it for a few minutes and came up with a solution. She told Megan about her best friend, Scott. We knew Scott in passing but never talked with him. She said he was very outgoing and he would probably go with Megan. Megan felt relieved because she was beginning to think she was going to have to go alone.   S c o t t agreed to go with Megan. Megan and Scott met the day before the formal. They hit it off, and Megan felt comfortable going with him. We could not have gotten a more perfect day for the formal. The sun shone and it was fairly warm. Again, Megan and I asked friends to help us get ready. Megan and I really enjoyed wearing make up and looking good. They did our hair and make up as Megan and I talked about the upcoming night. Megan and I felt like models. Scott was a perfect gentleman. He was on time and bought Megan flowers. Megan liked them a lot. We all took an OSD van to the formal after we took plenty of pictures. The van had quite a few people because there are many sisters who live on our floor. There were at least four of us in wheelchairs and two or three people sat on the seat. We talked and Scott made us laugh singing some rap song. It took us about a half-hour to get to the place. There was not any trace of snow or ice to worry about anymore. We did not have to worry about bothering with heavy coats either. It was the end of April, but in Edinboro snow is a possibility any time of the year.

From the minute Steve and Scott met, anyone would have thought that they were long lost brothers. They had similar personalities, senses of humor, they were both very helpful and liked making us laugh. They looked alike too, except Scott has brown hair and Steve is blond. Also, Scott was a little taller than Steve was. We sat at the same table and did nothing but laugh. They kept telling jokes and acted all silly. Megan and I were hysterical. When it came time for presentations, Steve and Scott were making us laugh so much that we thought we would have to leave the room. We literally had tears in our eyes from laughing. Megan and I asked them to keep quiet because everyone was staring at us. Every time we tried to be quiet, we would laugh even more. It felt like the longest half-hour in the world. Right then, Megan and I were positive that the entire sisterhood hated us.

Scott and Steve helped us get our food. Like the last formal, the food was served buffet style. This time Megan could eat without pain. Megan asked Scott to cut her food for her. Steve was very used to cutting my food and feeding me. Scott and Steve then teased each other about feeding one another. We were all amazed about how much Scott could eat. Steve and I were old enough to have a drink. We each had only one because the drinks were expensive. Megan and Scott stuck to soda and water because they were only 20.

This place had much more space than the fall formal. Everyone could have a better time because we weren't all crammed together. The dance floor was also much bigger allowing more people to dance. A guy that I was friends with went with another sister who lived on our floor. During the years we flirted off and on. Nothing came from it because I had Steve and he had a string of girlfriends. However, he was quite attractive. He came over to me and started small talk. He asked me if Steve and I were going to dance. I explained to him that Steve was not into dancing. He commented to Steve about that. Before I knew it, Steve asked me to dance. I suppose jealously does it every time.

After our first dance, I felt bad for Megan. Scott went to talk with a friend in the lobby, and Megan was left at our table. So, I asked Steve to go tell Megan that she should ask Scott to dance with her. With little convincing Scott and Megan were out on the dance floor. The next song just happened to be "Wonderful Tonight" by Eric Clapton. Steve stood me up out of my chair and danced with me. Now keep in mind, Steve is 6'and I am only 4'11". We made quite a sight. I barely came up to his stomach. I looked over and noticed that Scott had stood Megan out of her chair too. They looked cute together.

Megan is tall, but Scott was still taller than she was. They looked good together.

We all danced to many songs that night both in and out of our chairs. When we needed a break, we sat at the table, drank water and just talked. Steve and I did the YMCA and for one of the slow songs, Steve put me on his lap and we just swayed to the music. Megan and I had the best time. Steve and Scott enjoyed themselves too. All good things have to end and that included the formal. We piled back in the van and went back to the dorm around 12:15 AM.

Megan and I still talk about that night and have fond memories. We wish we could turn back time and do the night again. Now we only have a few pictures and our memories. Each time we hear "Wonderful Tonight" we are back dancing at the formal. Everything turned out perfectly. The guys made us feel really special. After that night, Scott remained a good friend. Unfortunately, Scott and Steve never saw each other again, but I bet if they did, the same silliness would come out immediately.

The following semester, fall of 1997, was going to be my busiest semester aside from student teaching. I had my junior field experience twice a week in a physical support classroom in Erie. I also took three classes in my major. The last president of the Organization for Disability Awareness stepped down and Megan and I took over. I was also the vice president of a national special education honorary. I had to draw the line somewhere or I would have gone insane.

So, I decided to go inactive in the sorority. Going inactive in a sorority meant the sister had to pay the dues, but did not have to meet the semester's service obligation. Before you go inactive, you must write a letter stating your reasons. A sister could go inactive when her workload became too much, but not two semesters in a row. I figured this would be the best idea because it would have been the most time-consuming of my activities.

Megan thought hard about going inactive as well. She just became vice president of a sports program for students with disabilities and the vice president of ODA. She was also taking five courses in her major. Besides, in the sorority, we really only hung around together so she did not want to be involved if I was inactive. So, we went ahead and wrote our inactive letters and went inactive.

As we predicted, the semester was extremely difficult. My field experience went great until the end. My supervisor and cooperating teacher gave me a low grade with no real reason other than my disability. Becoming a teacher with a disability has been far from easy. My academic advisor and our organization advisor became very ill and passed away ten days before the end of the semester. He was young, and he was also very supportive of me teaching. Megan got very sick a few times during the semester. In October, her left arm, the one she uses the most, had a severe case of tennis elbow or something and lost all feeling. She could move it, but not feel it. She had to go home and missed Disability Awareness Day. She also had very difficult courses. It was the roughest semester that Megan and I had to go through.

When the next semester began, Megan and I were not looking forward to going back into the sorority. We discussed quitting the sorority. We liked some aspects about the sorority such as the service projects. On the other hand, it was very stressful. Everyone talking about each other and the ridiculously late meetings every Monday night turned us off. We surprised all of our friends by being in the sorority. It was just not us.

We decided to attend one meeting and then make up our minds. Megan and I went and we were not happy. Everyone was bickering back and forth and the meeting went on much longer than necessary. We both knew that it was time to quit. The hard part was telling people. We thought that people would hate us.

The other sisters were not mean about us leaving. They understood our reasons and didn't ignore us. To our surprise, they actually seemed sad to see us go. To quit, all we had to do was write a letter explaining our reasons for leaving. Do we regret leaving the sorority? No. It was a good experience for both of us and we had fun. However, we both knew we would be better off leaving.

Megan and I had our experiences with romantic relationships and the opposite sex. We both analyzed our own relationships and each other's. In the next chapter we will explore our ins and outs of love.

Our Relationships
by Jessica

A common stereotype is that people who have disabilities do not or cannot have romantic relationships. This is false. People with disabilities have the same need to be loved, wanted and cared for like everyone else. We also can love, want and care for someone else. People with disabilities have romantic relationships, get married and have children. Another misconception is that disabled people only date disabled people. This is also false. People can date whomever they want, with or without a disability.

Like anyone, getting a date can be difficult. Some people can't see the person, and become fixated on the disability. Appearance influences people when they choose someone to date. Someone's appearance is the first thing people notice. When you have a disability, you have to show the world that you are capable too. Despite wheelchairs and whatever else, the true person is underneath. Unfortunately, many singles with disabilities are overlooked.

Dating as a teenager is difficult enough, but add on a disability and it is much more difficult. Megan and I both lacked dates in high school. During high school, other teenagers may not think it is the in thing to do by dating someone in a wheelchair, even if they look like a model.

The best way to end this line of thinking is to get children at a young age exposed to all kinds of people including people with disabilities. Learning about and being around people who have differences makes it much more difficult to discriminate against them.

During our college years and after graduation, Megan and I have spent many hours discussing romance and relationships. We talked about our ideal man and relationship. We even discussed what kind of wedding we would like and our future families. Our children's names were picked out and changed several times. Megan and I are both highly romantic. We could probably make a fortune writing romance novels. I cry at most heart-warming romantic movies. Megan cries at them once in a great while.

Megan and I grew up dreaming about happy endings and hoped that we would find Prince Charming one day. As teenagers, we read all the romantic stories about women finding the perfect man and living happily ever after. Unfortunately, the real world is not that simple. Dreams do not always come true no matter how much you may want them. However, it is important not to let go of dreams and keep reaching for them.

I have had some more experience with serious relationships than Megan. I am not certain why this is, but I guess I had more opportunity to meet people. From the time I was little, I always had this fascination with men and romance. My dad would often tease me, saying it was not normal for me to be so interested at such a young age. I remember being glued to the TV when Princess Diana and Prince Charles married. I also wanted to marry the star actor in The Greatest American Hero. I suppose it's the romantic side of my personality. Megan also longs and dreams for the perfect man and relationship. However, we know that wishing for perfection can only cause false hope.

My first relationship happened when I was fifteen. It is hard to actually say it was a relationship because I was young. It was my first experience of romance. My family had a Commodore computer, and one day my Dad introduced me to a new program called Q Link. My dad works with computers so I always was kept up-to-date with new software. I am positive that if Megan had this system at home she would have loved Q Link too. My dad later regretted introducing me to this because it ended up costing him a lot of money.

With a computer, modem and this program, people could connect to a system and chat with many people all at once. This was quite the tool for a 15-year-old teenager with a disability. In 1990, I started high school and had a little difficulty fitting in and finding friends. I was new to the school district and the only student with a significant physical disability. So, Q Link was like a gift from God.

My dad let me use this program for one hour a week. I would save this hour for Friday night. If possible, I would spread it out to all three days of the weekend. However, I used it mostly on Friday nights. Unlike now, when chatting over the Internet is free, Q Link cost eight cents per minute. For the first few months, I could control myself and remain at the one hour per weekend deal. Then I spun out of control. For Christmas one year, my parents gave me money to use on it. The computer was set up in my bedroom to make it easy for me to use. Maybe it was too easy for me. I am not proud of what I did, but within a few months, I jacked the bill up to almost $1000. I became almost obsessed because there was this guy and other friends that I talked to on there.

Jason was older than me by a few years. He was the first guy who truly accepted me despite my cerebral palsy. Unfortunately, he also lived in Jacksonville, Florida. Every night, I would wake up between two o'clock and five o'clock in the morning to speak to him. We had so much to talk about and he wrote me poems. Somehow I managed to stay on the honor roll at high school. We were boyfriend and girlfriend despite that we lived a thousand miles apart.

After my dad figured out what I was doing with our phone bill, Q Link ceased, and our relationship turned into letters and phone calls. My parents grounded me, and I never felt guiltier in my life. I did meet Jason when I went to Disney World with my mom and sister a few months later. Our relationship survived ten months, but like most long distance relationships, it did not survive. I was also a bit young for anything so serious. Jason and I continue our friendship through email. He is still a good friend of mine, and he is still living in Florida.

My next relationship happened right before my 17th birthday. I no longer had Q Link, but I owned a small laptop computer and modem. Before the Internet was all the rage, people had bulletin boards on their computers. They were usually free, if the phone numbers were local. A computer bulletin board is when a person sets up a communication system on their computer and people call in. People could write email to one another and post messages on different topics for everyone to see. Only one person could call in at once unless the owner had multiple phone lines.

During the summer of 1992, I called these bulletin boards because mainly people my age ran them. I also believe that Megan would have been interested in bulletin boards if she had the opportunity to use them. I found calling boards was a good way to meet new friends. One afternoon in July, I connected to a bulletin board and started talking with Brad, the guy in charge of it. We talked on there for many days and even over the phone. A few weeks later, I also met his best friend, Steve, on another bulletin board. Steve and I got along better than I did with Brad.

We had an instant attraction and talked constantly on the telephone. Brad and I met but we only became good friends. After Steve and I met, he went to the beach for a week and we missed each other. I just liked him and we could discuss anything. We laughed together and talked about every day. On the day he returned, August 1st, we talked on the phone from seven o'clock in the evening to four o'clock in the morning. At 3:15 A.M. Steve asked me to be his girlfriend, and I accepted.

Our relationship was the typical teenage romance. We went out on dates during the weekend, and had a great time. We lived only twenty minutes apart. Steve drove a black pickup truck and my wheelchair fit perfectly in the back. Of course he had to tie it down. Steve had little difficulty accepting my disability. He would take care of me fine, but his friends gave him a hard time about dating a girl in a wheelchair. Sixteen-year old guys can be so cruel. I had a talk with him and said that if he could not accept me fully then I could not stay with him. Being accepted in a relationship is extremely important. For Steve not to accept me would not be good for my self-esteem or the relationship. Steve thought it over. He did fully accept me and our relationship went along smoothly until a sad day in October.

On October 8th, Steve's mom suddenly had a heart attack. She was young and relatively healthy so this was a surprise. We were all in shock especially Steve and his younger sister. Afterward, she fell into a coma for a month before she died. Steve and his mother were very close so it hit him hard. In fact, the whole family was close. Now their lives were changed forever. Unfortunately, Steve and his father didn't get along that great so it took some adjusting for everyone.

A death would change any relationship, but Steve and I were only together for three months. We were also teenagers. No one close in my family had died back then so I had no idea what Steve was going through. This was not a minor crisis to pull through. I helped Steve the best I could by being his friend and listening to him when he needed to talk. I felt helpless because I could not make things better for him. Steve changed tremendously after she died. I was trying to hold on to the old Steve with all my strength, but I couldn't. He became very dark and hostile. Everything I did seemed to make him upset and angry.

We broke up for a brief time in January. He was hurting me and making me feel terrible. I knew much of his behavior was a part of the grieving cycle. However, I found myself feeling miserable and not doing Steve much good. The break up was very difficult, but I survived. I cried for two days and drove my family crazy. I also ate a lot of ice cream and played mushy love songs so I could wallow in my pity.

Steve called a few days later, and we temporarily sorted everything out. He realized he was not acting nice and wanted to change. I reluctantly tried it again because I missed him and cared for him. Our relationships went pretty much back to normal with occasional arguments. In time, I learned to love the new Steve. We went to the senior prom together and had a great time. We graduated high school the same year too. Then in August of 1994 I started college six hours away and Steve stayed home. He had no desire to go to college.

When I left Steve, it felt like part of me was being left behind. I missed him so much. He did come up and visit me a lot the first semester. Steve and Megan became friends. However, each semester the visits became a little less because of his work and my schedule. I had to keep up with my courses and obligations. Steve did not go to college, but he became an Emergency Medical Technician (EMT). He also has his own business selling various technologies. Our arguments grew when I left. We were becoming two very different people, but our love was still strong. So, the cycle would continue. We would argue, break up and make up again and again.

College breaks were enjoyable, but they were hard as well. Steve had his life, a very busy one, and managed it well. When I came home, I did not quite fit in his life anymore. We continued to try. Steve and I felt immense love, but our personalities and lives clashed. On November 17, 1995, Steve picked me up for Thanksgiving break. He also proposed to me. I knew we had our differences, but I thought that we could make it work. I happily accepted. Immediately, Megan and I hunted down wedding magazines. I asked her to be in my wedding and she agreed on the condition that I didn't make her wear pink.

We did not want to be married right away. I needed to finish my degree, and Steve had to make money and establish a stable career. However, as time went on, I tried discussing the wedding and the future. Every time I mentioned marriage, Steve froze and said we'd discuss it later. His new attitude had me concerned. I would stop talking about the wedding for a few weeks or months. However, he did not want anything to do with the wedding.

One day, in June 1997, Steve sat me down and told me that he did love me but did not want to marry. He said possibly later in his life, but he liked his life how it was. I was crushed and angry. Ever since I met Steve, I considered him to be "the one." I knew we fought, but we would always make it work. I also felt embarrassed. I felt like everyone was going to say how I could not keep a man. Of course this never happened. Above all my feelings, I felt incredibly sad. Steve made me feel safe with him and loved. Steve loved me unconditionally and I know that is hard to find. I wanted us to work so much.

Steve and I remained friends for a while after that. Remaining friends was more of a struggle for me. I kept on thinking that Steve would snap out of it and realize that he did want to marry me. I still loved him; but then again a part of me will always love him. Our relationship gradually fell apart over the last year. We talked less and saw each other only once in a while.

Currently, we talk occasionally. I got on with my life. I grew up and I know what I want in a relationship. I had to take time to get over him and learn who I was. I did it though and I'm happy. After my college graduation, Steve and I tried the dating scene once again. However, it only left me miserable after he started seeing some girl behind my back. That was the lowest part of my life, and I was depressed for awhile. Of course, he came back with all the apologies in the world, but I wised up and made a life for myself.

Megan and I have had our share of friendships with the opposite sex. Many of these friendships, we would have liked to become relationships. Some relationships did work out romantically, but many did not. However, despite the lack of romance, great friendships came about. Megan and I try to have relationships, and I think that is the important part. We never give up trying.

Since Megan never had any real experience with guys or flirting, I took it upon myself to teach her. I often sat in Megan's room giving her flirting tips. She would practice them to me and to herself. I helped her pick out outfits, hair styles, and some make up tips. I never had a younger sister so I enjoyed helping and giving her advice. Megan also helped me by listening and picking out clothes. We had fun, and it did pay off to some extent. We got dates and it seemed like we knew what we were doing.

During our sophomore year, Megan became friends with this guy, Paul, at college. They rode the van together to go to a class. Paul and Megan got along well and enjoyed each other's company. Paul was funny, talkative and outgoing, qualities that Megan looked for in a man. It took Megan awhile to admit that she liked him a bit more than a friend. Megan eventually gave him a card for Halloween to express her feelings. She liked Paul and wanted him to make a move. She was happy because he seemed to like her too.

Paul finally asked Megan to go to the movies with him on campus. Every weekend, at the University Center, they would show a movie. Many students went because there is not a whole lot to do in Edinboro. On the Friday of the date, Paul told her he could not go because he had too much homework. He told her this only hours before the date. Megan was so disappointed. She liked him and looked forward to the date. I felt mad at him for disappointing her. Megan and I also had doubts about his homework excuse.

Paul apologized, and a few weeks later, asked Megan out again. Megan accepted, but warned him not to stand her up or cancel again. If he did, there would not be a third chance. He assured her that he would not do that again. They picked another movie to see on a Friday. My friend, Grace, and I went to the movie as well. We sat in the back so in case Megan was having an awful time, she had a place to escape. Paul and Megan sat in the front.

Megan had a great time at the movie. She did not need to be rescued, and he did not cancel. Lucky for him, because if he stood her up, Megan and I could have caused bodily harm. Paul and Megan talked and laughed. Paul turned into a gentleman. He helped her with her jacket both taking it off and putting it back on again. He also walked her back to her room. No, he did not kiss her, but that would be rather pushy to do on a first date. Megan successfully survived her first date.

Unfortunately, nothing romantic came out of their friendship. They occasionally talked but their friendship eventually faded away. Megan really hoped for a boyfriend. She just wanted someone special in her life. I tried to point out men I thought Megan would like on campus. However, she did not find them interesting or they had girlfriends. In our junior year, Megan's love life started to pick up again.

After our first sorority formal, Megan became interested in her date, Aaron. He was a few years older than Megan and was preparing to graduate the next semester. Grace had set them up for the formal. They had a good time together at the formal. They almost danced at the formal, but it was time to leave. He also kissed Megan on the cheek at the end of the formal.

Aaron gave Megan a card after the formal telling her how much he enjoyed himself. He acted interested in her. When we came back from the winter break, Aaron called Megan again. They would occasionally talk on the phone. She was really beginning to like him, however, she could never tell the way he felt. He seemed to like her, but he did not follow through when he said he was going to call. His calls were sporadic.

One weekend, Aaron asked Megan if he could come

over to watch a movie. He had gone over to her dorm a few times before. Megan wanted to go out to a place with him instead. She wanted her friends to meet and get to know him. I decided to go to the bar that weekend with a few friends and suggested she invite Aaron. Megan thought it over and decided it would be a great idea. Aaron agreed. Megan felt very excited, but she had a strange feeling something bad was going to happen. I thought Megan was just nervous about the date. I tried to assure her everything would be fine.

Megan's uneasy feelings were correct. Aaron showed up late, and to top it off he invited another woman. He hardly talked to Megan and when he did, he talked down to her. He flirted openly with the other woman. He had no respect for Megan's feelings. Megan felt very hurt, humiliated and disappointed. Her friends and I felt total rage and could not believe he acted that way. Aaron called Megan a few days later, but his behavior disgusted her and she refused to speak with him.

Megan needed a few months away from the dating scene to heal from Aaron. She thought he liked her, and they could have relationship. Megan and I spent time sorting out her feelings. I wanted her to understand that it was not her fault. I hoped that she would not give up on trying because he acted so horribly. She did nothing wrong. He did lead her on, but to this day we don't know his reasons, other than the fact that he was a jerk.

After our second formal, Megan again became interested in her date, Scott. Our friend, Alyson, set Megan up with Scott for the formal. Scott had an excellent sense of humor and he was outgoing. They also had a good time together at the formal. Megan and Scott talked some on the phone afterwards. He also went out with us to celebrate Megan's 21st birthday. Megan was pretty shy and had a difficult time responding to Scott that night. We did have a good time though. After her birthday, we discussed the possibilities of them dating.

Unfortunately, Scott only wanted friendship. Megan tried to get him interested in her romantically, and Scott showed some interest, but it was only friendly flirting. This also took Megan some time to get over because to her Scott was a great match. Everyone thought so. However, one cannot create feelings that are not there. I believe that is the hardest lesson in life--when you like or love someone and they do not feel the same.

Through the Internet and Resort, Megan met and became close to some more men. She met one guy, Dan, she truly cared about on the Resort. Dan and Megan discussed everything and got along great. They cared very much for each other. He lived quite far and was in the process of moving even farther away from Megan. He was beginning medical school in Los Angeles and could not use the Resort anymore. On his last night, Dan told Megan not to be too sad, that if their relationship were meant to be, it would be. Megan saw Dan a few months later on the Resort but has not spoken with him since then.

Megan met another special guy on the resort, Alex. Unfortunately, he also lived in another state. Alex and Megan became friends almost immediately. They talked on the Resort and in email almost every day. Megan helped him with problems and vice versa. Megan found it easy to trust him and was comfortable confiding in him.

They exchanged pictures and Megan's disability did not phase him at all. They see things differently, but this makes their friendship even more interesting. Alex had some serious reservations about online relationships because he had had some bad experiences with them and he warned Megan about them. Megan and Alex correspond via email and Internet chats. They remain very good friends, but nothing more.

My dating life slowed down after Steve and I went separate ways. Men interested in me during my engagement had met other people. I did see a friend for two weeks, but it did not last. We were way too different, but we are still friends. Friendships are important. For a few months, however, I became very interested in one guy. He did not go to Edinboro, he was not in Pennsylvania and in fact, he does not live in America.

I designed my own web page concerning teaching, my interests and cerebral palsy. I created the page in August 1997, and made it to meet new people and practice using the Internet. On my page, I had a guest book so people can sign on and write a comment if they would like. I set most of it up during the summer and made minor changes during the semester. I would check the guest book for any new messages at least once a week.

One day in October, Megan and I were using the web. I decided to check my guest book to see if there was anything new. I began to read a rather long entry from a man in the Isle of Man. Megan and I teased about the name Isle of Man by saying we sure would like to go there. I continued reading. His name was Tyler and he was from London, but went to school in the Isle of Man.

He wrote that he was becoming frustrated with college, was ready to give up, but then he came across my page. My page motivated Tyler to keep working to obtain his degree. He said I could write him email if I wanted.

I was taken back at first. His words were passionate, and I could tell he meant what he said. He was thanking me for keeping him in college. I had no idea that my web site could help someone. I contemplated writing him back, and I figured I should because he took the time to write me. I could at least write him back and let him know I got the message.

Before we knew it, a very profound friendship started over email. Both of us had busy schedules, but found time to write. I began to look forward to his letters. From the start, Tyler had no doubt in his mind I would make it as a teacher. He never pitied me because of CP. He thought it was just an asset to my life to make me the person I am.

One night I was talking on the Resort like I did every night before bed. Out of the blue, somebody asked me if I was the same person that they had bookmarked for the web. At first, I was not going to answer because I thought they asked the wrong person, but then I replied and said I did not know. Then they asked if I knew someone from the Isle of Man. My heart stopped and then started to beat wildly. My mind was racing. Could it be Tyler? I said yes and I quickly learned it was Tyler.

Tyler and I went in a private area and started talking. We could not get over that we actually met on there too. Megan had also signed on to the Resort and I told her whom I'd just met. She was surprised too. For many nights we would meet on the Resort. The more I knew him, the more I wanted to know. There is a five-hour time difference between us. Tyler would wait up to all hours of the night to talk to me.

During Christmas break, Tyler stayed at the Isle of Man. We would talk whenever we had a chance. Before we even realized what was happening, Tyler and I fell in love. Right before college started again, I went in the hospital for a test to see if a certain medical procedure would help me. It was for the baclofen pump, a device that releases a steady stream of medicine into my bloodstream to control my muscle spasms. I went in January 6th and was out the next day. I could not sleep too well the next night. The test required a spinal tap. For those of you that have had a spinal tap, you understand how I felt. If you've never had one, just picture a needle in your spine. They hurt and can cause severe headaches. Tyler and I talked on the Resort and our feelings came out. He told me I was the key to his heart and hopefully we would be together one day.

Tyler and I never made a serious commitment. We knew what we felt. We talked on the Internet as much as we could. Presently, we cannot meet as often as we would like. He graduated with a degree in Marine Biology and is looking for jobs. We even talked on the phone, but we have to be careful about that because phone bills can get high. Ironically, he could understand me fine and I have trouble understanding him due to his English accent. After I graduated, I talked to Tyler once more and then never heard from again. I know he is alive and well because I met his girlfriend on the Resort one night. I wish him luck and happiness. I will never forget our chats and email.

After I came home from college, I was ready to start making friends around my area. I was also ready to start dating. I signed up with several services that matched personalities with other people over the Internet. I knew all the dangers of online matchmaking and didn't enter into it blindly. I played it safe. My responses were tremendous. Everyday I would get at least 10 or more emails from prospective dates. I tried to respond to all of them, even those whom I knew I didn't want to date. I felt it was polite. I met some really nice people. However, I didn't hit it off with anyone. I enjoyed meeting new people and building my career at the same time.

One particular day I received a rather lengthy email from a guy who lived close to me. I read the email with a big smile on my face. I thought to myself that he was the one I'd been waiting for. In the email, he described himself as having high morals, pro-life, fun, outgoing and honest. I liked the way he wrote and felt an immediate connection. Then I read the end of the e-mail. He said that he was an atheist. I felt stunned because he wrote with passion about life and a love of people. In my experiences, the atheists that I'd met seemed a little cynical and pessimistic. This was new to me.

Since I am Catholic and love my religion, I knew we wouldn't go any further than friendship. I wasn't about to give up my religion for a relationship. God will always come first in my life. I wrote Israel back giving him my web site address. On my web site, I give information about myself, including information about cerebral palsy.

I thought that if he was still interested, he'd write me again. I really didn't think I would hear from him again.

The next night I was on the Internet and all of the sudden I got an Instant Message from him. I had no clue who it was, but I said hello. He introduced himself as Israel, and asked me if I remembered him. The name sounded familiar, but I had received so many e-mails since then that I wasn't very sure. He said that he visited my web site and liked it a lot. We talked a lot, and had several things in common. Israel gave me his web site address to check out. I visited his site and it had tons of information. I found out we were Rush Limbaugh and Dr. Laura fans. I also noticed that we were both fascinated by computers. Because of the amount of information on his site, I decided to bookmark it and look later. To this day I still haven't seen it all.

Israel and I chatted on the Internet every night. We became friends over the Internet and I couldn't wait to talk to him each night. His high intelligence intrigued me. He seemed to know a little bit of everything. Our conversations ranged from our romantic tastes to religion. Religion was our biggest debate. We discussed religion for hours, and I never seemed to become bored.

Israel did ask a few questions about my cerebral palsy, but he never seemed scared by it. I was honest with him and answered all his questions to the best of my ability. After a few weeks, we decided to talk by phone. I wasn't comfortable with giving out my number so he gave me his. It was around two o'clock in the morning, and we decided to carry our religious debate over the phone. I felt nervous about calling because of my speech impediment.

I was scared that he wouldn't be able to understand me or wouldn't like the way I talk. My speech isn't that bad, but I have a tendency to slur my words especially when I'm nervous. Luckily, Israel understood me fine and told me that my voice sounded beautiful to him.

Israel and I met in person and we got along great. We started seriously dating in June, and have been together ever since. We love, trust, and help each other. This last Easter, Israel was confirmed into the Catholic church. We are now planning to be married in the near future and want to start a family. Megan likes Israel too and she is going to be a bridesmaid in our wedding.

Megan met a few men since graduation, but nothing serious has happened yet. She is still seeking the right relationship. She thought she met a good guy to date, but suddenly he wasn't interested anymore. They corresponded through email, Internet chat and by telephone. We think he realized he couldn't handle the disability factor. Megan moved on and is still looking for the right guy.

Finding someone can get frustrating and difficult, but she hopes that it will be worth the effort. She wants to get married and have a family. Megan and I will always support each other and be there to listen through our different relationships. After all, supporting each other is what best friends are for.

Through our relationships, Megan and I managed to get out and have fun. Megan will now share our experiences at concerts we attended together.

The Concert Event Of A Lifetime...

by Megan

I have always been a country music fan. Jessica never has. In fact, she laughed at some of her friends when they even mentioned a Garth Brooks concert when she was 16. Like most people, she had the perception that all country music was about the dog dying, the woman leaving, and the truck breaking down all on the same day. But she quickly learned that if she was going to spend any time in my room, she would have to learn to deal with country.

At first, she couldn't stand country music. I'd have to turn my stereo off whenever Jessica came to visit. Then she would just tune it out whenever it was on. Jessica would often come over to my room after classes. We would sit and talk and have a snack. I always had my stereo or CMT videos on. After a few months, she realized that not all country music was as bad as she thought it was. Eventually, she got to the point where she could tolerate it and even liked some of it. She even bought some county CDs.

Jessica really liked one particular country singer. Garth Brooks. She bought me the video of one of his concerts for Christmas 1994. It almost killed her to buy a country video, and it embarrassed her when her friends saw what she was buying, but she did it. We watched it together one Friday night.

After we watched the concert, Jessica couldn't believe that she had refused to go see him live. I had seen him in concert once before but wanted to go again. We decided that we were going to go to a Garth Brooks concert if he ever came anywhere near Erie. We couldn't really make any plans to go though because, obviously, we had no say in his tour schedule.

We kept it in the back of our minds that we wanted to go someday, but couldn't really do anything about it. We also didn't really keep track of his tour and where it was going to be. When our sophomore year started and all the new freshmen moved in, I went around and introduced myself to them, like Jessica had done when we were freshman. There was one girl who was a Garth Brooks fan. Actually, she wasn't just a fan. She was a fanatic. She kept track of all his tour dates, his personal appearances, everything. You name it, she could tell you. She promised to tell Jessica and me when Garth Brooks came anywhere near Erie.

In February of 1996, on a Thursday, she told us that Garth Brooks was going to be doing 4 shows in Cleveland in March, a scant two hours from Erie. I immediately told Jessica and we both started thinking of ways we could get there. About an hour later, I called my mom and asked her if she would drive me there. She said she would. Then I casually slipped in that Jess wanted to go to. She said she'd have to think about it and get back to me.

My mom called me back the next day, a Friday. My younger brother had decided he wanted to go. Since he was going, he could lift Jessica in and out of our van and her chair. A friend of his was going to go too. With five of us going, Jess and I decided who was going to get to take their electric chair. Only one electric chair would fit in our minivan along with one manual chair. We decided that Jessica would take hers because her manual wheelchair is not very comfortable for long periods of time.

On Saturday morning, after we were up and ready, both of us sat in Jess's room, both with phones. I had brought over my cordless phone to call. We had decided that Jessica would put all the tickets on her credit card and the rest of us would pay her when her bill came in. At 10 AM, as soon as the ticket offices opened, we started calling. Neither one of us was getting through, so we enlisted the help of others. Jessica called her dad, her boyfriend, and her sister and had them all calling for us. I called my mom and had her call. Jess and I were calling as well. We had six people calling and trying to get us tickets. Jessica even said a prayer.

About an hour after we started and about ten minutes after her prayer session, Jessica's boyfriend called her and told us we could quit trying. He had gotten us five tickets for the show on Saturday, March 23. There wasn't much else we could do after we got the tickets but wait for the day of the show to come. When Jess got the actual tickets in the mail, she had me put them up in a safe place where I'd know where they were later. We went about our business and everything went along smoothly. Until the day of the concert, that is.

That morning, my mom called me and told me that my

brother's friend had decided that he wasn't going. My dad said he would go, but he wouldn't drive the van. He wanted to take his car. That meant that neither of us could take our electric chairs. Jess and I called everyone we knew to try to find someone else who would go with us so one of us could take our electric chair. We didn't have any luck.

I called my mom back and she told me when they would be there. My house is exactly two hours from our dorm in Edinboro. Jessica and I went to the cafeteria and ate lunch, did some homework, and got ready to go all while my parents were driving up to get us. Jessica was working on a project for her field experience and I was finishing a project for my Children's Literature class. When my parents got there, my dad took the tickets and we were off.

My dad picked Jessica up and put her in the car. I couldn't help but laugh. It looked kind of like my dad was holding a baby. He's 6'5" and Jessica is 4'11". It was a sight. When I started laughing, so did Jessica. And we laughed all the rest of the way to Cleveland. My mom threatened to sit between us and separate us because we were giggling so much, and my dad said he was going to leave us on the side of the road. I guess our constant giggling can get pretty annoying at times.

We stopped about an hour outside of Cleveland to have dinner. It was quite an experience. Jess had to take her chair in because she can't sit in a regular chair. My dad walked me in. That got us our first set of strange looks. Jessica and I just looked back, and my mom told us to behave. The next set of strange looks came from the bewildered waiter. He looked at me and then at my dad next to me. Then he looked at Jess and my mom next to her, asking her the easiest way to feed her. The only one the waiter could make any sense out of was my brother. He got us our drinks and came back with the menus. He gave one to everyone but Jessica and me. Then he looked at my dad and asked him if we knew how to use menus. He, like a lot of people do, automatically associated the disability with a mental impairment. My dad just shrugged and told him he'd have to ask us. That kind of frazzled his nerves. Poor guy. Our waiter really earned his tip that night.

When we were on the road again, Jess and I started singing along with the radio. My dad listens to oldies. Oldies are perfect to sing along to, as we'd done many times before. After a while, I think it started to annoy my dad because he turned the radio off. So we just sat back and watch the trees go by until we got into the city. When we passed the Rock and Roll Hall of Fame and Museum, my dad told us we were almost there. Jessica asked what lake was there, and I laughed when I told her we were still on Lake Erie. When we actually got into the city, Jessica laughed at me because I kept looking out the windows to see everything. She'd been to Philadelphia many times, but at that time, I hadn't really been to any city when it was light enough to see.

We found the arena and went to find a place to park. We parked in an underground lot. The guy who parked the cars let my mom, my brother, Jess and me stay in the car. He made my dad get out while he parked. He took off at probably about 60 mph or more in that garage. My mom warned him that if he scratched the car, my dad was not going to be happy. Neither Jessica nor I have really good balance, so were being tossed around in the back seat. We were giggling hysterically, so was my mom, and my brother was in the front seat yelling at us to be quiet.

When we were finally safe in a parking spot, we all got out of the car and found our way into the arena. We crowded into an elevator with about twenty other people who just kept pushing until Jess and I were literally pressed up against the back wall. My brother and my dad finally told some of them to move so we at least had room to breathe. We got off on our level and decided we'd buy T-shirts or whatever we wanted before the show started. My brother helped me stand up so I could see what they had and my dad lifted Jess up so she could see. When we had decided, my mom went up to buy them while we went and found our seats.

We were in the very top two rows. Jess and I were sitting on the floor at the top where the seating for disabled people was. My mom was sitting in a folding chair beside us. My dad and brother were in the row below us. Jess and I sat there and watched the wannabe cowboys come in and go out. They really impressed Jessica. You don't see many cowboys, real or wannabe, in the city. When my mom came back, she had a Coke for us to share while we waited for the concert to start.

The show started a little bit late. When it started, my mom stood up behind Jessica and me. My dad really didn't do anything but sit there. Jess and I were singing along. We couldn't really see anything on the stage but shapes because we were so far. I had my dad's binoculars.

I tried to hold them up so Jess could see, but with my arm being kind of unsteady and her spasms, that was kind of dangerous. My mom tried too, but Jess said she could see fine.

About halfway through the concert, we became aware of the boy sitting beside us. He had Down's syndrome and he was so excited to be there. He would yell out "Hey Garth Brooks! It's me, ----------------!" We were not making fun of him at all, but Jessica and I started doing the same thing. We thought it was rather cute. No one but my mom and dad could hear us. My mom told us again to behave ourselves, but she was laughing while she said it.

When the show was over, Garth came out for an encore. We stayed for that one. When he came out for another encore, my dad said we were going to leave so we could beat the traffic. None of us wanted to and we all complained because we were going to miss his cover of *American Pie.* But my dad said we were leaving then or it would be 45 minutes before we even got out of the parking garage. He was right, too.

We all got our coats on and hiked back to the car. About halfway back to Edinboro, Jess and I started to get really tired. My brother was asleep and my mom was dozing off. Jessica and I started to play Mrs. Parson's Picnic. She started because I had never heard of it before. I had played that game, but never heard it called by that name. She would say the name of a picnic item starting with the letter A, and I would have to repeat it and add one starting with B. And so on and so forth. Because it was so late and we were so tired, and also because of our speech impairments, it took almost the whole drive back to Edinboro. And we only got through about three-quarters of the alphabet.

When we got to Edinboro, my dad got Jess out of the car and my mom took her inside to the PC room. It was almost one in the morning, but I had to continue on home because my aunt's bridal shower was the next day. After the shower, I went back to school.

After the concert, Jessica and I discussed the fact that we'd like to go to more concerts together. Unfortunately, we both liked very different types of music and Garth Brooks was really the only artist we both liked. That discussion led to an experiment for one of my psychology classes. Jessica was convinced that country music subconsciously depressed me, and I was adamant that it didn't.

We decided that I would listen to only pop music for two weeks and that she would listen to only country. We had told friends about this so they could watch for any personality changes in us. The experiment didn't last for more the 36 hours. The next night, a Friday, a new Melissa Etheridge video came on VH1 and we ended up watching the entire Top Ten Countdown. So there went Jess's part in the experiment. I had also forgotten to change the station on my clock radio, which I have on when I go to sleep. That ended my part and the entire experiment was over.

We couldn't really go to anymore concerts because our tastes were so different. We also had no way to get there, since neither of us can drive. Shortly after our failed experiment, Jessica started listening to the Rolling Stones while I was in her room. Of course, I hated them at first. Eventually, though, I started to like some songs. I even borrowed her CDs and taped them.

In the first month of our senior year, Jessica flew home to go to her second Rolling Stones concert. She came back and told me all about it. Since I had taped her CDs and liked the music, some of it anyway, I decided that I'd like to go to one of their shows if it was possible. We didn't think much more about it though.

That same month, we heard that Garth Brooks was going to be in Pittsburgh in October. It was just a rumor when we heard it, but I looked it up on the Web and found out that it wasn't just a rumor. We even called to see how much tickets would be. Then we started to ask everybody we knew if they could take us. My dad said it was too far for my mom to drive in one night, and none of our other friends wanted to miss any classes. We thought about renting one of the accessible vans and a driver from the Office for Students with Disabilities to take us down, but it would have been around $300 or $400. So we didn't get to go.

In November, Jessica and I were playing around on the Web, watching Rolling Stones video clips. We pulled up their tour dates just to see if they were going to be anywhere near Erie. The closest they were going to be was Syracuse, NY, in January of 1998. Once again, we were bound and determined that we were going to go. Jess had never been to a country concert before she saw Garth Brooks and I have still never been to a rock concert. She wanted to take me because she said that you couldn't get any more rock than the Rolling Stones.

We checked out ticket prices and the distance and driving time from Edinboro to Syracuse. Then we started to ask people if they could take us. We asked everyone we knew who liked the Stones. I asked my mom if she could take us. I even asked my little brother, because he was old enough to drive by then. He said he might, but my dad wouldn't let him.

A couple of our friends who worked as PCs (personal care attendants) at school said they would really like to, but the concert was only a week after we came back from Christmas break. They would have been out of work for a month. So that left them out. Nobody really wanted to drive to Syracuse in the middle of January, anyway. Jess has already seen the Stones. I might go see them if they tour again, which is highly likely.

After I graduated, I heard about a Garth Brooks concert in September 98 in Buffalo. Jessica and I discussed going to it together, but she wasn't sure about her student teaching schedule and I wasn't sure if my family could pick her up. Jessica decided not to go. Meanwhile, my mom, brother and aunt decided they would go with me so I bought tickets. I got them for the last weekend in September on a Friday night.

September came in no time. Unfortunately, my dad had a meeting and my mom had to go with him on the same weekend of the concert. My aunts and brother decided not to go. So, I was stuck with four tickets to a Garth Brooks concert and no way to get there. I told Jessica the situation and she said that she would like to go and would ask around to see if we could get a driver. My mom said that we could use our van if we could find someone to drive it.

Jessica asked our friend, Alyson, if she would like to go to the concert. Alyson was a huge Garth Brooks fan. She jumped for joy when Jessica asked her. Now we needed one more person to go. Alyson asked her best friend, Rebecca, to go. Rebecca is also a big Garth Brooks fan and agreed to go and she had a friend that could go too. So, we were all set. I planned to visit Jessica that weekend, and Alyson offered to help me with care.

The weekend finally came. We were all very excited. My mom dropped me off at Edinboro about 45 minutes before Jessica returned from teaching. Jessica left her key in the personal care room so I could put my stuff in her room. When she got home, Jessica quickly changed before we met Alyson and the girls. We all piled in the van and away we went. The concert was about an hour and half away so we picked up food at Burger King and sang Garth Brooks songs along the way. I fed Jessica, and we managed fine despite the moving vehicle.

We arrived at the arena with little difficulty. We parked, and went to our seats. Our seats were way up top but we could see everything perfectly. We watched all the men in their cowboy hats and boots. We saw one man that could have been Garth's twin. The opening artist was Trisha Yearwood. She put on a great show. Alyson and Jessica shared a beer before Garth Brooks came on stage. The lights dimmed and the crowd went wild when Garth Brooks came on stage. We sang, clapped and hollered during the concert.

On our trip home, we were still hyper, but a little tired. We talked and sang with our very stressed vocal chords.

When we returned to our dorm, we were laughing hysterically because when you open the side door to the van it sounds like a little man singing. It took us about 20 minutes to get out of the van because we couldn't stop laughing. Jessica and I got to bed about 3:30 in the morning.

That was the last concert Jessica and I went to together. Hopefully, one day we will get to go to another concert together. If we do, I am sure that it will be an adventure.

Next Jessica will share our summer school experience together. We had a lot of fun that month in school, and it's something we will never forget.

Summer School
by Jessica

Many college students like catching up on credits or want to go to summer school. The classes are two to four hours every day for a certain number of weeks. The work comes at a high pace, and there is much to be covered and completed. I always thought of attending summer school, but since I lived six hours away, the idea just didn't go anywhere. Also, during the summer, the Office for Students with Disabilities did not offer any support services like personal care and academic aides.

In 1996, Megan and I wanted to go to summer school. We both were behind in credits so we thought it would be good to go to school in the summer. For Megan, going to summer school would be easier for a few reasons. She lived closer to Edinboro so it would not be hard to get there. She also can do things more independently than I can. Megan would only need someone to come in the morning and help her get dressed. She would also need someone to help her with the laundry and some other minor things.

I need more help during the day. So, finding help would be much more difficult. I do not need help continuously all day. I need it for the bathroom, eating, dressing and so on. The best way to handle the situation would be to have someone live with me. I could have someone come in at certain times of the day. Megan also offered to help me in any way she could. I had a lot to think about. I also lived six hours away, and my dad would have a lot of work packing me up for just one month of school. I needed to consider all of these things.

I discussed the situation with Grace. We are very close friends who also met during freshman year. She is also a special education major. Grace told me that she would be interested in living with me and taking classes. We could take the same courses, but I would need to find someone to help me physically write during tests. I would pay her for her physical help like anyone paying a caregiver. We would live in the same dorm so she would be available whenever I needed her. We needed to work out the details, but it sounded like a great plan.

My father and I discussed the details. He was not too excited. We were a pretty close family and I was away all year. I explained to him why summer school was important. I also made it clear that I would be well taken care of. He agreed, but wasn't happy. He understood it was something I wanted to do though.

Megan discussed summer school with her parents. They understood her reasons as well. Megan asked her friend, Erin, if she would help her in the morning. Erin worked as a personal care attendant and didn't live far from Edinboro. They worked out the payment details. Everything was settled. Megan and I were going to summer school the month of June.

Now it was time to put the summer school plans into action. Grace and I chose our courses. We took Social Psychology and Dynamic Earth. Megan decided to take the course, Dynamic Earth, with us. She also took a literature course. I asked a friend who was also taking courses to help me write my tests. She agreed. Now we just had to wait for the semester to finish and summer school to begin.

Unfortunately, Megan and I had a disagreement the end of the semester. I do not remember what happened, but we had some hard feelings toward each other. We didn't talk during the break before summer school. That was extremely unusual for us. We used to call once a week. At that time, Megan didn't have an Internet account at home so we did not have contact that way. I missed Megan, but I guess we thought our separation would be best.

The few weeks away from college went by fast. Before I knew it, Dad and I were making the six-hour trip back to Edinboro. Grace helped me move in. We arranged the room so that we would each have half of the room. I had never had a roommate before, except for my sister, so I was really skeptical about how everything was going to fit. Our things did fit and we were ready for the month.

Megan moved in the next day. She just got back from California. She had a medical procedure done to improve her physical function. It did help some with her speech and balance. Whenever we saw each other in the hallway, we became tense. I did not know what to do because when we left I thought Megan didn't want to talk to me. Eventually, the more we saw each other, the more we talked. Megan and I had a talk to clear the air. We made it through yet another disagreement.

I liked having a roommate. My sister and I shared a

bedroom for many years so I was used to living with someone else. Grace and I had to be flexible and understanding, but for the most part things worked out smoothly. We both had boyfriends so we needed to work out the phone usage. We did not have any fights and got along well. One weekend, Grace's parents took us to Lake Erie. We had fun on the beach and enjoyed getting off campus for awhile.

Megan and Erin also got along well. Erin came for five days a week. She would stay for an hour and help Megan with whatever she needed. On the weekends, another personal care attendant would help Megan. This was so Erin could have a break on the weekend. When Grace and I ate in the cafeteria, Megan would often come with us. Grace would help Megan get her food. The Office for Students with Disabilities tried to get a meal aide but was not too successful that summer.

Since Megan and I cleared our disagreements up, we began to hang around together again. We would all walk to Dynamic Earth together. Between the three of us, the professor had his work cut out for himself. We sat in the front and all had a sense of humor. Unfortunately, when one would think something was funny, we all started laughing. Megan and I got yelled at during a movie about earthquakes. For some reason we found it very humorous. The professor asked us to be quiet. We all did well in the class.

During the weekend, Megan and I would go out and explore the town of Edinboro. We would eat lunch and sometimes dinner at either Burger King, McDonalds, Pizza Hut or Perkins. We would also watch a movie in town or visit the local grocery store. Deciding what to do was not too difficult because Edinboro is a small town. One Saturday, Megan and I decided to walk all over town. We found streets we did not know existed. It was so much fun. The weather usually stayed comfortable, but once in a while it became too hot for even us to trek all over.

Grace did not mind when Megan and I went on our little adventures. Grace would rest, catch up on homework or see her boyfriend. Grace and I had our outings as well. We often ate at Taco Bell in town for lunch or dinner. On Father's Day weekend, her parents came up and took us to Lake Erie. We played on the beach. I got sand everywhere. We ate at Eat n Park afterwards. Grace has a friend that lives close to Edinboro. She invited us to her house. We had fun, but it was a little difficult to get in and out of the house. Sometimes Grace and I would rent movies and just stay home. Videos are good for rainy days.

Grace colored my hair one day. We were bored and she offered to do it. So, Megan and I went into town and picked up hair stuff. Megan found it amusing that I took forever to decide the color. I chose auburn. Grace put me in a chair and did the coloring process in the sink. Megan watched, took pictures and kept me company. My hair came out fine.

Thunderstorms scare me a lot. I hate lightning like you wouldn't believe. So, during the summer Megan and Grace patiently helped me deal with these storms. I would make Megan sit in the hallway with me. At night, Grace tolerated my jumping at every lightning flash.

The days went by fast. We were surprised how fast time flew. Before we knew it, the month ended. I was happy to go home, but I had a great time with Grace and Megan. It felt good to be outside all the time and just to be close to my closest friends. Looking back on it, I would have never thought all three of us would actually do that. I am very happy we had the opportunity.

Close Encounters Of The Bar Kind

by Megan

Shortly after Jessica turned 21 in August of 1996, we decided that we would venture into town and go to the bar. For a small town, Edinboro has an amazing number of bars. We had heard people talking about the various bars in town and decided to go to the one that was notorious for not carding people before 9:00 PM. This practice was bad for business, but it was good for Jess and me because I was only 20. All of her friends that she really wanted to go out with were still only 20. So we decided to try it and pray we didn't get caught. If we had, I would have gotten into a lot of trouble and her teaching career would have been over before it started.

The first time we went was a fairly warm night in late September. We always had to plan to go out on a warm night if we were by ourselves because neither of us can take our jackets off that easily. I think that was one of the most trouble-free nights we had at the bar. We didn't run into any strange people and we weren't approached by any weird barflies.

We got all ready to go and met in my room because I was going to do Jessica's makeup for her. Neither of us had asked the other one what she was wearing and when we met up, we were wearing almost identical outfits. Jeans, black lycra tops and denim shirts. Jessica and I talked about one of us changing clothes, but decided against it because we wanted to get there before 9:00 so we didn't get carded.

When we got there, the place was almost completely empty. It stayed that way for most of the night. There wasn't a lot happening that night, so Jess and I just sat in a corner with our drinks and talked.

When a couple of guys came in and sat fairly close to us, we got our first clue that you should never mix draft beer and mixed drinks. Someone as tiny as Jessica shouldn't anyway. One of the guys that was sitting by us was drinking a really dark beer. Before I even knew what she was doing, let alone have time to stop her, Jessica went right over and asked him what kind it was. He was very polite and told her it was Sam Adams. She got her answer, came back to the table and was perfectly happy.

After she finished her drink and had about half of mine, we decided we better go back to the dorms. That's when we found out that Jessica really shouldn't have mixed draft beer and vodka. As soon as we got outside, all kinds of questions started pouring out of Jessica's mouth. There is an apartment building about five minutes from the bar. She turned into the driveway and asked me if this was where we lived. I said no and finally convinced her to keep going. As we were going down the sidewalk, she asked me if I was her sister and if I knew where her boyfriend was. I didn't mean to laugh at her, but I couldn't help it.

The last house before the campus starts had a party

going on. Jessica was pretty convinced that we should stay and go to the party. When we finally got back into the dorms, our RA (resident advisor) was working the front desk. Normally, Jessica had to stay with me while I signed us both in. But we got in and she asked me for permission to go to the restroom. When the RA heard that, I think she wanted Jessica to go to bed as soon as possible. So she let her go while I stayed behind and signed us in.

The next morning, Jessica had the worst headache. She wasn't really sick. She just had a headache and had lost her voice from trying to talk over the music. We decided we weren't going to try the bar again for a while. We did end up going again soon after that. Not by ourselves though. Jessica's sister Hannah had come up for a few days in October and wanted to go out. Even though it was cold out by that time, we could go because Hannah would be there to help us with our jackets.

That was the last trouble-free night we spent at the bar. We went to the same one for a while. We had our drinks and were sitting at the bar talking. I was talking to this guy who had recently graduated from Edinboro. Apparently Jess and Hannah thought we needed to be able to talk without them around because they both got up and spent about 15 minutes over at the jukebox. When they came back, the guy's friends had shown up. We all talked for a while and listened to the music Jess and Hannah had put on the jukebox. Then the guys left to do their own thing and the bar started filling up with really odd people so we left.

We weren't quite ready to go back yet so we went a

little further into town to another bar. We got in with no trouble, but we didn't stay very long. It was really crowded and filled with smoke. Jessica and Hannah also wanted to get me back to the dorm because they thought I had finished my drink too fast at the other bar.

In the middle of February, Jess's sister came up again to visit Jess. There was this guy from near where they lived that Hannah had met at Edinboro and liked. Jess and Hannah and I went out with him and another guy. Well, they met us at the bar.

We had a few drinks while we waited and Hannah tried to teach me to play pool. I didn't do very well but I had fun. After the guys came, Hannah spent a lot of the time talking to the one she liked. Jessica had hoped I would like the other guy so we talked a while, but didn't really hit it off.

So Jess and I went out to the dance floor. We were talking to each other and to the guys in the band that was playing that night. When the band got off their break and started playing again, we started dancing. We weren't really paying any attention to the people around us. We didn't even notice the guy in the black leather jacket that was watching us. He must have been at least 35. He was really scruffy-looking and was so drunk he could hardly stand up. The band started into their next song and Jess and I started dancing again.

Out of nowhere, this guy just came over to Jessica and kissed her. I don't know why he did it. I just know it scared us both. If I had been thinking straight, I would have grabbed the controller on her wheelchair and backed her up. But I didn't. I grabbed the collar of his coat instead and pulled with everyone else. It took four guys from the bar and the guitar player from the band to pull him off her.

Then we had to go tell Hannah what had happened. She was outraged, but the guys didn't even seem to care. She went and talked to the guy, but I made her go back and sit down with her sister before she started a fight. We didn't leave right away because we didn't want the guy to think he had scared us off. But we left about 20 minutes later.

We went to the bar again at the end of February. My friend Aaron was supposed to come over to my dorm room that night, but another friend was going to the bar for the first time with Jessica and I wanted to go. We had already arranged for our friend Erin to meet us there, so Jessica felt relatively safe going. So I arranged just to meet him there.

Our first clue that the evening was going to go bad was the songs on the stereo while we were getting ready. It was supposed to be somewhat of a date for me and Aaron, even though there was a whole group of us going. The songs on the radio were all heartbreak songs. Then on the way there, I got unexplainably nervous and Jessica got one of her patented feelings that something was going to happen. And if that wasn't enough to clue us in, the song on the jukebox when we went in was Garth Brooks' Victim of the Game.

But we were there and determined to have a good time. We were having a great time. About a half an hour after we arrived, Aaron got there and everything went downhill. He was already partially drunk. He hardly even spoke to me and when he did, he talked like I was 5 years old. He spoke more to Jess and Erin than he did to me. They both just gave him very short, curt answers and disgusted looks.

He had been there about a half an hour when a mutual friend showed up. She was really drunk. You could tell just by looking at her. You could also tell when she said she had already been to every bar in town. As soon as she got there, I might as well have left. Aaron paid absolutely no attention to me or anyone else. He did everything with this woman except have sex with her on the bar, seemingly oblivious to what he was doing to me. I just sat there and watched, totally humiliated. Jessica and Erin were ready to kill him. And our other friend was sitting there taking it all in so that she could spread it all over the dorm when we got back.

After about an hour of this, Aaron and Chelsea decided they were going to leave and go to another bar. He asked Jessica and me if we wanted to go but we declined. When he asked, he put his arm around Jessica. She just stiffened up and thought about faking an arm spasm so that she could hit him. But she didn't and he left.

We stayed a while after that to finish our drinks, but we saw the man who had kissed Jess come in, so we left. And I never heard from Aaron, or Ratboy as I call him now, again.

Hannah came up again the next week because it was her spring break. We all went to the same bar. I wasn't really up for it, but I went anyway because Jess thought it would be fun. I was miserable. I hadn't expected it to be hard to go back there and it shouldn't have been, but it was. I didn't even finish my drink. I just waited for the rest of them to finish and then we went home.

Jessica and I didn't go out again until the night of my 21st birthday in August of 1997. We went with our friends Alyson, Carly and Scott, the guy I really liked at the time. It was a disaster. We got there and I got really shy. Not nervous, I just wouldn't hardly speak to Scott. I was so scared of what he would say if he knew that I liked him. He bought me a drink for my birthday and talked me into doing a shot with him. Jessica and Carly also bought me a drink for my birthday.

One of the odd people who always seem attracted to me and Jessica also bought me a drink. He called himself The Gimp although he walked fine. He bought one for Jessica too after he sensed that we were not real crazy about him hanging around our table. Another friend of ours showed up and bought me a drink for my birthday. She worked at the school as a personal care worker so she offered to take Jess and me across the street to the accessible restroom in Burger King.

When we got back, Scott had decided to go to another bar with his fraternity big brother. So he did. And we walked home with Jessica telling me to be quiet because if she heard me crying she would start and then we'd all be in trouble. She also didn't want Alyson or Carly to hear me because she knew I didn't want them to know I liked Scott.

We went to the bar together for the last time on the night after Halloween 1997. We were fine on the way there. We saw other people we knew out walking and could talk to them. We got to the bar and immediately wanted to leave. There was no one there that we knew and it was extremely crowded. But we decided to stick it out. Neither one of us even had a drink because it was too crowded to get to the bar. So we decided to leave.

It took us almost 15 minutes to fight our way through the crowd and to the door. When we finally got outside, it seemed like the whole town was deserted. Walking home, we saw no one at all and there was no one walking with us. Every other time we had walked alone before, we had been fine. This time was different, though. We just kept repeating over and over, like some sort of mantra, "I wish Scott was here" or "I wish Steve was here." We have never made it from town back to the dorm as quickly as we did that night.

Another time we went to a bar, my chair decided to break down half way back to campus. The weather was extremely cold and it was snowing. For a long time, no one was around and people in cars just zoomed by. Jessica stayed with me, but she was beginning to wonder if she should go back to our dorm to get help. We discussed options and huddled together to keep from freezing.

Luckily, a police car came and they asked if we needed help. We told them what happened and they radioed the PC room to get help. A personal care worker from the men's side came and pushed me to our dorm. We were so cold.

That was the last time we went to the bar together. Jessica went with other friends up at school. When I went to visit, it was too cold for us to walk. I'm sure we'll go again someday. Maybe on one of our vacations or if we end up living near each other. We'll just have to try to avoid the weird people.

Jessica and I always wanted to take a vacation together, and we finally got to. Our adventures on that vacation follow.

And EPCOT Will Never Be The Same

by Megan

A vacation together is the truest test of any friendship.

In our sophomore year, Jess and I decided that we were going to take a vacation together sometime before we both got out of school and parted ways. We probably decided this in January or February, when it gets down to about 15 degrees during the day in Edinboro.

It was more of Jessica's idea that we go to Florida, to Disney World. I would have been just as happy going to the Jersey Shore or to Ocean City, Maryland, because I haven't really been to the beach since I was a kid. Living in the northwest corner of Pennsylvania, not really close to Erie with Presque Isle or anywhere else for that matter, doesn't really afford a lot of opportunities to go to the beach. Plus, I didn't really think we could pull it off. I know better now.

We had both been to Disney World before, Jess when she was 15 and me when I was 14. But we wanted to go back. Probably because no one (at least us) ever really outgrows Disney. And Jess always goes to the beach because she lives right close to it. We decided that Disney would probably be more fun than the beach anyway.

Following the pattern that we have of planning major

events before we know if we can do them, we planned the entire trip that night sitting in Jess's room. For a couple of weeks, we talked and planned who we were going to take with us to help us and what we were going to do down there. The talking continued, but we never did anything about it.

As the semester wore on, and Jess got more involved in her first field experience and I got busy with my classes, our plans for the trip kind of drifted away. We still talked about it off and on but never very seriously. We had decided whom we were going to ask to go with us to help us. We had even decided how we would pay for ourselves and another person. But, again, that's as far as it went. No serious plans were made.

Then came our junior year and we got even busier. Jessica was involved in Sigma Pi Epsilon Delta, a special education honors fraternity, and that took up time. We both had classes, and we were both pledging Gamma Sigs. Jess was involved in more, but we were both pretty busy. Because of that, the Florida trip was still discussed in detail but no plans were made. It continued this way through the first semester of our junior year.

In the beginning of 1997, everything got more hectic. We had both made it into the sorority, Jess was VP of Sigma Pi, I was involved with the Rolling Scots and I had just declared a major, at last. We were both swamped with work and different activities. We were also fighting a losing battle for the girls who lived on our floor in the dorm. That stressed us out even more. I don't think the trip got much attention that semester, except when we both said we wished we were there already.

That summer while I was at school, I asked my friend Erin if she would be interested in going with me when we finally made the plans. She said she would try her best, but didn't know for sure. She wanted to start school again and didn't know if she would have any extra money. Jess and I started talking about it more seriously after that, over the phone and over the Internet. I think she mentioned it to her sister that summer so that Hannah could start saving the money she would need if she went.

When we got back to school, our plans kind of drifted off again. We had just taken over as president and vice-president of the Organization for Disability Awareness and were trying to build it back up from the ground. We both had classes and Jess had her junior field experience at a school in Erie. I was also the vice-president of the adaptive intramural sports program on campus. We were inactive in the sorority but we still had more than enough to do without worrying about planning a vacation.

We did talk about it, though. The weather was unusually warm for Halloween night in Edinboro, so we went out wandering through town to have dinner and meet some of our friends who were helping trick-or-treaters cross the street. While we were eating our pizza, we once again planned the entire trip. Only this time we planned what it would be like if we were taking the guys we liked at the time. We both knew that wasn't going to happen, but it was fun to talk about. Then we went off to meet our friends, one of whom was the guy I liked, and everything went downhill from there. Professors started piling on the work, we were trying to plan a fund-raiser for ODA, and we had just learned that one of our friends and the club advisor was fatally ill. That was really hard for Jess because he was her academic advisor and favorite professor.

After break when everything calmed down and got back to normal, or at least as normal as it got around there, we started to get serious about going to Florida. I asked my friend Erin again and she said the same thing. She would do her best but didn't know for sure. We even picked out dates for the trip that would be good for everyone.

Then Hannah got involved and everything got rolling.

Jessica's sister is great. The first time she visited Jess at school I felt like she was my sister too. Hannah is three years older than Jess and she's like Superwoman. She's just a ball of energy. She had her heart set on going with us and I guess she got tired of us talking about it but never doing anything.

She got on the phone and called all kinds of travel agents. She basically did all the legwork. She called and found us the best deal on a package. She made sure the room and all the facilities were accessible for our chairs. She even convinced me that she could help both of us if I wanted. I wasn't sure because she's so much smaller than I am, and helping both Jess and me can be quite a bit for one person. The travel agency was already jacking up the price and we couldn't wait for an answer from Erin, so Hannah booked the trip the next morning. And I told Erin that I'd invite her to go next time we went. She was a little disappointed because she wanted to go with me and I wanted her to go, but she understood.

So after two years of talking about it, we were finally

going to get to go to Florida.

We booked the trip in the first part of April for the week of May 18-21, 1998. After the trip was all set, we couldn't believe that it was only a month away. Jess and I talked about it every night, discussing different plans of action and trying to figure out how we were going to fit in a trip to Pleasure Island. We planned about 500 different ways to hit all the parks in four days.

About a week after the trip was set up, everything started to get really hectic again at school. Jessica was worried about where they might place her for student teaching in the fall, I was worried about not being able to do an internship before I graduated, and we were both worried about Awareness Day. Awareness Day is a day when anyone on campus can come out and try different wheelchairs and adaptive equipment and learn about different services for the disabled. ODA had held an Awareness Day in October of 1997, and it was a success. We had our suspicions that getting people outside of ODA involved in the organization of the day might not be the best idea, but we had them help anyway. Our suspicions were confirmed on Awareness Day. It was pretty much a loss, and that just added to our end-of-the-semester stress.

I went to Virginia with the Rolling Scots, the weekend before finals, which added greatly to my stress. I competed in the Mid-Atlantic Wheelchair Games in air rifle and qualified for the Nationals in September 1998. The weekend was fun but stressful for me. It gave Jessica a lot of time to study though. Then came finals week. We were both stressed, but happy because those were the last finals of our undergrad careers.

After finals were over on May 9th, we parted ways for the time being and both went home for a few weeks. Jess went home to get ready for Florida and look for a summer job. I went home and finished planning and buying stuff for my cousin's bridal shower on May 16th.

After the shower was over, my mom helped me pack everything because we had to drive down to Philadelphia to meet Jess and her sister at the airport. None of us even thought of the Pittsburgh airport. Pittsburgh is just about in the middle between our houses. It would have been a little farther for Jess's dad to drive, but not nearly as far for my mom as it was to Philly.

My mom and I left home at noon and got to our hotel around seven o'clock. We called Jess to let her know we were there and to get directions to the airport and to where we were supposed to meet them from her dad. We all had to get up at five or five-thirty in the morning because we had to be at the airport at least an hour and a half before our eight o'clock flight. We had to get there earlier than most people because they had to load our chairs on the plane and get us on before everyone else.

First class wasn't full and it's a lot easier to get us in and out of, so the airline bumped us up on the flight down. The airline people took our chairs and let Jess's dad and my mom put us on the plane. We got all situated in our seats and said goodbye to our parents. Jess and I sat next to each other. Hannah sat in front of us. When our parents were off, everyone else started to come on. When everyone was on the plane, we were finally off to Florida.

All during the flight, we kept saying how it didn't even

seem real that we were going. After all our talking and planning, we could hardly believe that it was really happening. I don't think either one of us believed it until we actually got off the plane in Orlando. We talked and ate breakfast during the flight. I had to feed Jessica because Hannah couldn't reach behind her too well. That in itself was an adventure. I think the crew that cleaned up the plane found a few of the strawberries I attempted to feed Jess on the floor under our seats. Luckily, our chairs were the same as they were when they went on the plane. I was a little worried about that because mine is not a typical wheelchair.

We had to wait for everyone else to get off the plane before Hannah and the flight attendants could help us get off. Waiting was a little difficult because we were all ready to get going to the parks. When we were off and back in our own chairs, we went to find our luggage. After quite a hike around the Orlando airport to find the baggage terminal, we went to get our van to the resort. The driver was very friendly and helpful.

It took about a half an hour to get to the Caribbean Beach Resort where we were staying. We got there and checked in to our room. The room wasn't ready yet, so we dropped of our luggage and headed to the new Animal Kingdom. Buses come every twenty minutes to take people wherever they need to go in Disney World, and they are all accessible.

We caught the bus to the Animal Kingdom and got there around two o'clock or so. It was packed. Hannah stopped for a few minutes to cover us in sunscreen and then she was off. She went a mile a minute. Jess and I are in motorized chairs and we could hardly keep up with her. But we managed to stay fairly close to her and not lose track of her. She took pictures of everything by itself and pictures of everything with us in front of whatever it was. We saw all the attractions and rode the rides and saw some awesome shows. In all the parks, people with disabilities can usually get on the rides first. That makes it nice because sitting in the sun for hours on end in a wheelchair isn't very healthy. Almost all of the rides were accessible, but most could only take one wheelchair at a time. Hannah usually transferred me out into a seat and let Jess stay in her chair because I have better balance than Jess does.

By the time Hannah suggested that we eat something, we were all starting to get worn out and starting to get hungry because we hadn't eaten since we had breakfast on the plane. When we went to eat dinner, Jessica was starting to feel a little bit sick because she wasn't used to the heat yet. She was fine after she had something to eat and a cold drink. That's when it became clear that we were going to face a mini-disaster a day. That's typical for me and Jess though. Almost everywhere we go or anything we do, there's some kind of problem.

When we got back to our hotel around 9:30 that night, we wandered around for about an hour trying to find our room. The resort was huge. We finally found someone to point us to the room, and we went and unpacked. The room was gorgeous. Then we went out and wandered around a while longer trying to find a soda machine. We did and found our room again on the second try. Hannah called for a wake-up call and we were all out like a light.

The next day we were going to the Magic Kingdom. After we were all up and semi-ready to go, we made lunch reservations at Cinderella's Castle for noon. We caught the bus to the park and got there around 11 o'clock. We walked around a little and rode It's A Small World. Then we went to lunch. Hannah took a picture of Jessica and me with Cinderella and we went up to the restaurant. It was beautiful inside. We had a huge lunch, more than what we usually eat. After we had our fill of food and of everyone calling us m'lady, we went back out into the park for the rest of the day.

Everything was going good. We were getting on rides with very little trouble. And when Hannah did have trouble transferring me, probably because I'm so much taller than she is, there was always someone willing to help us. About halfway through the day, our mini-disaster hit. We were on the train that takes you around the park, out in the middle of the park and nowhere near the station where I had left my chair, and my contact lens fell out.

It couldn't have landed on my leg so that it would have been clean enough to put back in. It had to land on the floor so that I couldn't put it back in. I picked it up and held it until the train pulled into the station and I got back in my chair. Then I rewet it with my eyedrops and tried to put it back in. But my hand was too covered with sunscreen. So we walked around for a while until we found a place to wash my hands and I got my lens back in. So that crisis was under control.

At the Magic Kingdom, Jess and I were like kids. Hannah kept trying to persuade us to stop for a while and eat dinner. But we didn't want to take the time to slow down. We finally convinced her that since we had eaten a really big lunch, we were set and could wait to eat until we were watching the fireworks that night.

And that's what we did. We ate miniature pizzas while we were watching the fireworks at the park that night. After about 14 hours out in the park, we were exhausted when we got back to the resort. Needless to say, we all got a really good night's sleep that night.

On Wednesday, we were supposed to have breakfast with the characters as a part of our package. We got ready to go and caught the bus to the Boardwalk where the restaurant was. Our mini-disaster struck early that day. After we got to the Boardwalk and I was getting off the bus, the lift broke about a third of the way down. I sat there on the lift about a foot off the ground for about a half an hour. The drivers finally fixed the problem and got me down. Then Jess got off and we went to breakfast.

Hannah got pictures of us with all the characters that were there. She even got her picture taken with her favorite character, Goofy. After breakfast, we went to one of the gift shops on the Boardwalk. They were selling Beanie Babies really cheap. Jess and Hannah collect them and wanted some. I, personally, don't see what the big deal is. Then we headed off the MGM Studios.

Our disaster had already hit us, so we were free and clear. We rode the movie rides that we had time for at MGM and walked around the park and saw some shows. We had to get two parks into the same day. So about halfway through the day, we headed over to EPCOT. As soon as we got there, Jess's sister wanted to redo my ponytail. We headed into the nearest building and were almost inside when we heard Jessica and some little boy laughing hysterically behind us. Jessica was trying to tell us something but she was laughing so hard we couldn't understand her. We looked up and we were headed into the men's restroom. We changed course and went to the right place, redid my hair, and we were off again.

Hannah again tried to get us to take a break and eat dinner. Once again we reasoned that since we had eaten a big breakfast, we were good until the fireworks show. We explored all the different countries, mostly England though. Jessica has a really good friend in England and wanted to know somewhat what it was like over there. In a sweet shop, we spotted a package of cookies that would be called sandwich cookies over here. In jolly old England, they're called Digestive Creams. Jess and I started giggling and couldn't stop. Everyone in the shop turned around and stared at us. We were still laughing when we watched the fireworks. We didn't really ride many rides, only one, because by then we were all kind of tired of transferring and being transferred.

As soon as it started to get dark, we found places to sit and watch the fireworks. By then we were all getting hungry, but we couldn't get into any of the English pubs that were closest to where were wanted to sit. So Hannah went and tried to find us pizza or hamburgers to eat. But she couldn't find anything so we dined on strawberry yogurt, chocolate eclairs and Coke while we watched IllumiNations.

When we got back to the hotel, we packed everything we could before we went to bed. The next day, our first disaster hit early. The zipper on my duffel bag broke and it wouldn't close. We had to call the bellboy to duct tape it shut for the flight home. We planned to meet at the Animal Kingdom later in the morning. Hannah had to check out and she wanted to give everybody some time by themselves. Jessica and I waited outside for the bus, but it didn't come for an hour and a half. By the time we got there, we only had about ten minutes before we had to meet Hannah for lunch.

After we ate, we went and bought all our souvenirs there. We had decided to do that so we didn't have to carry them around all the parks and so we could just take them as carry-on bags. We got back to the hotel just in time to catch our ride back to the airport. We got there and checked on our flight. The seating had been messed up so we were all bumped up to first class again.

We went through the same routine of getting our chairs on and getting ourselves on. Then we waited for everyone else to board and after months of planning and too short of a time there, we were leaving Orlando. Jess and I giggled almost all the way back to Philly. Even the flight attendant commented on our giggles while we were waiting to be taken off the plane. The airline let my mom and Jess's dad get us off the plane.

After we got out of the terminal, Jess's dad and sister went to get our luggage and we told my mom about the trip. And that was that. We got on the elevators and each went our own way. Jessica and Hannah went an hour home and my mom and I drove the six hours back to our house.

After all that, our vacation in Disney World only exists in pictures and memories now. While we were down there, Jess and I decided we'd like to make this a yearly thing. We may be able to pull it off, at least every other year. We'll have to wait and see.

Life After Graduation
by Megan

I have been out of school for a year and a half. Jessica has been out for a little over a year. We both graduated in the same ceremony on December 19, 1998. By that time, though, I had been finished with all my classes and degree requirements for almost six months. So I didn't really feel like I was graduating with Jessica, who had been finishing her degree requirements by student teaching. But it was fun to do anyway. I got to see all the people, students and professors that I hadn't seen since the regular semester had ended in May. And, of course, I got to see Jessica, if only for a short time. We wanted to at least be able to talk for a minute because we really had no idea when we'd see each other again. She and her family left almost immediately after the ceremony because her father wanted to get on the road before the snowstorm that was brewing hit and made the roads more treacherous than they already were.

We each went our separate ways home and our years at Edinboro had officially come to an end. I went back to work on Monday and Jessica started looking for jobs and looking for a full time position. Jessica took her final National Teacher's Exam and passed. She also ended things with Steve for good and dated some guys. I guess those months were not very eventful, for me, because I can't really remember anything that happened until April. That was when Jessica flew back up to Edinboro to visit Alyson. Alyson had two more semesters before graduating. I convinced my mom to take me up to Erie for the day so I could meet Jess at the Millcreek Mall because, once again, we didn't know when we could get together again. We had fun and got to spend a few hours together. Of course, we laughed a lot still.

We had planned to go on another vacation together that summer to Busch Gardens Colonial Williamsburg. But the plans fell through almost before they even started to form. My cousin, who lives in New Mexico, was due to have identical twin boys in April. I wanted to go see them but I also wanted to go on vacation with Jessica. Because of my job and finances, I could only do one trip. As much as I wanted to spend time with Jessica and her family, I hadn't seen any of my family in New Mexico since I was 13 years old, so I opted to go out there. Jessica and I plan to see each other soon but we have to work out details. One day we would like to return to Disney World. And, no matter how hard I try or how much I save, my bank account never seems to get any bigger. Jessica has been dating a guy for months and marriage plans for them are in the future. So there may be a wedding or wedding plans that might help us get together. We will have to see.

We did get to see each other the summer after we graduated. Jessica came up to Bradford and spent a week at my house in July. We figured that would be a lot easier than me going down to her house because my dad has made the first floor of our house completely accessible. Although we didn't do a whole lot of anything, we had a great time. Jessica went to work with me for two days and volunteered at the agency's preschool summer session and I took two days off. We played a lot of board games, usually Disney Trivia. We went to McDonald's one day before we went to see the South Park movie and discovered that the McDonald's in my town is horribly inaccessible. My family reunion was the day before Jessica went home so she went to that with us and had a so-so time. The reunion was in a pavilion in a park outside. In the middle of the afternoon, there was a thunderstorm. Jessica is absolutely terrified of thunderstorms especially, as we know now, when she is outside in one. If she had jumped any more or gotten any closer to me, she would have ended up in my lap. But we all survived. We had a great time that week. Even though it was a few months ago, it seems more like a few weeks ago.

The World Of Work

During the winter, Jessica volunteered to take over the design and upkeep of my personal web site for me. She had developed a real talent for HTML language and web design and she knew that I was fairly technologically impaired and computer illiterate. I figured that letting her mess around with my page would stop her from redesigning her own page every two days. Other people who had begun asking her for help soon noticed her talent for design. As a hobby, Jessica started designing pages for friends. Her hobby soon turned into a full-fledged, one-person business. Jessica's Web Design is still up and running and probably will continue to operate until Jessica finds a full time teaching position. Until then, though, it's a way to keep busy and a way to make money. She also writes articles for web sites and teaches online courses.

Jessica received her teaching certification papers in October 1999. She had been supposed to receive her official certification in February or March but there was a screw up at Edinboro. Apparently, the Dean of Education didn't sign in the right place or he didn't sign at all. That meant that Jessica couldn't seriously consider any full time jobs. Now that she has her certification, she can seriously consider and be seriously considered for positions.

As for me, I'm stuck in a post-college quandary. I have been stuck there since about January of 1999 and see no signs of getting unstuck anytime soon. I still have no idea what I want to do. Except write. My writing has been the one constant, the one thing that I've always known I wanted to do. It's not easy to find a job as a writer though. The job I have now is the closest thing to a writing job that I could find. I write newsletters, create posters and mailings, organize and publicize fundraisers and do some public relations for a small agency here at home. One of the best things about it is that I only work part time so that still leaves me with time to work on my writing. I just recently started to write articles for web sites.

I know there isn't anything wrong with not having my life all planned and organized by now, but I'm starting to feel left behind. All my friends started college with a definite idea of what they wanted to get a degree in and what they wanted to do when they graduated. Now they are all moving forward, looking for jobs, going to grad school, making plans to get engaged or married and I'm just sort of here. I started college with no idea what I wanted to be and I still am not sure. I have no plans to go to grad school, I am staying in the job I have now and I definitely have no plans to get engaged or married. I'm not even dating anyone. But I'm happy, for the most part, and I will be happy doing whatever I'm doing and I will hold onto the idea that my life will eventually work itself out for the best.

You may have noticed slight changes in the time frame this is written in. That's because Jessica and I had it written by the end of the summer of 1998. We wanted to have it written and most of the revisions done before Jessica started student teaching. We knew that she wouldn't have time to work on it after she started teaching. We have done a lot of rewriting and revising since graduation, though. Both of us have slowly remembered more and different experiences we had.

The rewrites and revisions have caused more fights and arguments than they are worth, in my opinion. A lot of the people who have read the various drafts would beg to differ with me about that. All things considered though (the fights, the arguments, the differences of opinion and the clashing personalities and writing styles), I think it was a great experience for both of us and I wouldn't have given it up for anything.

* * * * *